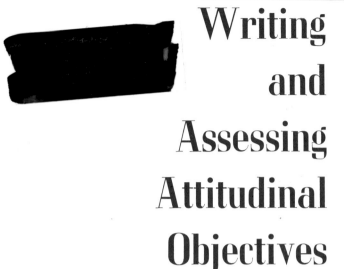

Writing and Assessing Attitudinal Objectives

Gerald R. Girod

Oregon College of Education

Charles E. Merrill Publishing Company
A Bell & Howell Company
Columbus, Ohio

To my wife, Linda

Published by
Charles E. Merrill Publishing Company
A Bell & Howell Company
Columbus, Ohio 43216

International Standard Book Number: 0-675-08921-2

Library of Congress Catalog Card Number: 73-77660

1 2 3 4 5 6 7 8 9 10 / 77 76 75 74 73
PRINTED IN THE UNITED STATES OF AMERICA

Contents

To the Instructor

This program is designed to teach students how to write behavioral objectives for attitude development and change. The taxonomical scheme used in the program is a "new-comer" to the list of educational taxonomies. Frank B. May, Washington State University, designed the taxonomy.[1] Briefly, May's *Modified Taxonomy* roughly parallels that taxonomy edited by Krathwohl.[2] The major difference is that May's taxonomy is written in behavioral terms while that designed by Krathwohl requires an inferential judgement by the observer.

Two assumptions have been made about the users of this program.

1. That users have already acquired sufficient information about behavioral objectives such that they could demonstrate comprehension skills in discussing behavioral objectives.
2. That users are not seeking methods to bring about attitude change from this program. These materials are not designed to train students in techniques of bringing about attitudinal change. Rather, they are designed to aid them in selecting and writing attitudinal objectives and measures in order to be better prepared to change attitudes.

The cognitive objectives for each chapter of this program are listed prior to the beginning of the chapter. It will be assumed that a user who progresses through the program will meet all of those objectives. Cognitive performance can be measured by an analysis of his post-test scores.

An individual can learn to write affective objectives and to assess student performance in terms of those goals by reading this text. There should be no doubt that the student will learn those skills and concepts more fully if he has an opportunity to use them. Employment can take the form of trying them out with his own students but the user will also need to discuss them minimally. There is no thought that this text will be sufficient for helping all students attain the goals of high level comprehension. Programing is useful to most students but so is the chance to state and defend one's opinions. Instructors will find it beneficial, then, to schedule some time to discuss with their students the concepts contained herein.

Hopefully, these materials will be of aid in future educational planning by the users. That was the major goal in the construction of this program.

---

[1] The taxonomy and the rationale behind its construction is discussed in *College Student Survey* 3 (Fall, 1969).

[2] Krathwohl, David R. et al., *Taxonomy of Educational Objectives, Handbook II: Affective Domain.* New York: David McKay, 1964.

To the Student

Teachers are generally given the responsibility for developing attitudes in their pupils. Work, self, science, school, our nation, drugs, and bicycle safety are a few of the multitude of topics toward which teachers are to facilitiate the acquisition of acceptable attitudes. Yet few people have been able to provide many useful ways of looking at attitudes to enable the teacher to tackle that job.

A few writers have provided some aid by preparing plans for categorizing objectives which teachers and curriculum agencies write. Others have attempted to define the attitudinal goals of various topic areas. The problem has always been that the concepts used by both groups have differed in name and the level of concept specificity has been low. Too often terms used have been so "slippery" that the user has been left holding an empty conceptual bag.

This text is designed to alleviate the problem, at least from the teacher's point of view. In the following pages you should learn some words that have a greater degree of clarity in describing attitudes. Additionally, you should learn how to categorize attitudinal objectives with a high degree of reliability. As a result of that learning you, as a classroom teacher, should have acquired sufficient skills to be able to state attitudinal objectives for your pupils and be able to assess in an efficient manner to what degree those goals were met.

The method used in presenting the instructional portion of the text relies heavily on programed instruction. Programing was chosen because it has one major advantage in facilitating instruction. As you read you will be forced to respond to that which you are to learn. A standard text is like a one-way conversation—the author writes and you read. In programing you are asked to take a more active role in learning.

Because learning seems to be facilitated when you are taught in an orderly, logical manner, it is suggested that you not skip frames in the text unless you are given that option in the directions. The text has been extensively tested with graduate and undergraduate students. The recommendation not to skip frames comes from a good source—other students.

A programed text is never designed to be the sole source in an instructional process. You will still need to discuss the material with others to check your perception of the content. Hopefully, the programed aspect of the text will decrease the amount of learning time. However, nothing can decrease the value in using your knowledge to communicate to others.

Prior to beginning work on the programed portion of the text, you'll be asked to respond to an attitude scale. After you've finished the text there will be another attitudinal device for you to complete. If the text met your needs, then your score on the second attitude scale should be higher. To determine whether the text worked for you a set of scoring directions has been included. Using those directions you'll be able to score your own scales and be able to match the scores on the first and second tests to determine if your attitude toward the study and use of attitudinal objectives improved. Hopefully, you will experience such a gain.

Preceding the programed section of each of the first six chapters is a short expository section. Those sections are designed to present a problem set. The programed section was constructed toward the goal that you will learn to solve the problem previously stated. By reading carefully the expository section you should clearly understand what it is and why it is necessary to learn from the content.

Chapter 7 is written using a non-programed format. That writing pattern was chosen because a shift in content necessitated a different style of communication. The final chapter is a blatant attempt to affect your attitude so that it will match mine.

B. F. Skinner, an advocate of programed instruction, has intimated that the world (and programs) should be structured so that learning is fun and easy. He's right. However, that's much easier to verbalize than it is to implement. In an attempt to make your learning more enjoyable, an attempt was made to include a wee bit of humor and an occasional anecdote.

Two outcomes are posited for this text. First, the reader who is or is preparing to become a classroom teacher should become independent in planning for and assessing attitudinal outcomes. No longer should you be dependent upon attitudinal devices which other educators believe useful. You should be ready to state goals as you choose and assess student attainment with devices you construct. As an outgrowth of that knowledge, the second goal should result. You should come to believe in your skill and in the value of dealing with student attitudes. If that second goal of increasing your confidence in yourself as a planner and evaluator of attitudes does not occur, then the text has failed.

How to Use This Program

The best way to use this program is with a "mask," such as a piece of paper, to cover the answer. For example, when you are working through a frame in the program, you will find a blank line to fill in or some directions for constructing an answer. Below the frame will be a wavy rule running across the paper. Below the line is the answer.

If you see the solution before you try to answer the question in the frame, your learning will not be nearly as effective. Do the following steps as you work through the program:

1. Place a mask on each page of the program as you begin the page.
2. Slide the mask down until you come to the wavy rule running across the page.
3. Answer the question.
4. Slide the mask down to the next wavy rule and check your work.
5. If your answer was correct, move on to the next frame—following steps 2 and 3 above.
6. If your answer was incorrect make sure that you know why the listed answer was correct. If additional directions are given to review prior frames, do so. Then follow steps 2 and 3 above.

Only one person has been so careful working through this program that they got all the frames correct the first time. Is that enough of a challenge?

Complete this test before *you read any of the program.*

PRETEST

Directions: Tear out the answer sheet that immediately follows this test. Read each item carefully. On the answer sheet circle the answer that best represents your attitude. Make sure that you mark the answer that corresponds to the item. Try to work as quickly as possible.

1. I would be willing to spend time reading about means of holding teachers accountable for the attitudes of their pupils.
   a. Very willing
   b. Willing
   c. Mildly willing
   d. Mildly unwilling
   e. Unwilling
   f. Very unwilling

2. In the past, how much time did you willingly spend studying about attitudinal objectives?
   a. No time
   b. Only a few minutes
   c. Twenty minutes
   d. Almost an hour
   e. More than an hour but less than two
   f. As long as necessary to thoroughly understand

3. How many minutes per week would you like to spend in planning for attitudinal development of your class?
   a. More than 3 hours
   b. 2–3 hours
   c. 1–2 hours
   d. 30–60 minutes
   e. less than 30 minutes
   f. no time at all

4. When you've run across articles during your leisure reading that have advocated educational accountability, how did you react?
   a. I haven't read any
   b. After a while I read one— but I disagreed
   c. Within a few minutes I started reading—but I disagreed
   d. After a while I read one— and I agreed
   e. Within a few minutes I started reading—and I agreed
   f. I began reading immediately—and I agreed

5. Would you be willing to actively participate in a curriculum meeting with other interested teachers in selecting ways to foster attitudinal development in your students?
   a. Very willing
   b. Willing
   c. Mildly willing
   d. Mildly unwilling
   e. Unwilling
   f. Very unwilling

ix

6. I have discussed with my fellow students or teachers techniques for assessing attitudes in children.
    a. Never
    b. Once—for about 10 minutes
    c. Once—for quite a while
    d. Twice
    e. Three times
    f. More than three times

7. If you were given a chance to work in a school where you were expected to demonstrate some attitudinal growth in your pupils, how long would it take you to decide?
    a. I'd say yes immediately
    b. A few minutes—but I'd probably say yes
    c. I'd need more information —but I'd probably say yes
    d. I'd need more information —but I'd probably say no
    e. A few minutes—but I'd probably say no
    f. I'd say no immediately

8. When you've had the chance in your spare time to read an article about teaching or assessing attitudes, how have you reacted?
    a. I haven't read any—and don't intend to
    b. I always intend to—but I haven't
    c. If I run back across them later, I do
    d. I've done so after reading the other articles
    e. I've done so within a few minutes
    f. I've done so immediately

9. Would you be willing to spend planning time writing attitudinal objectives?
    a. Very willing
    b. Willing
    c. Mildly willing
    d. Mildly unwilling
    e. Unwilling
    f. Very unwilling

10. How long has it been since you attempted to convince others of the merits of educational accountability for attitudes?
    a. I never tried
    b. Sometime this year
    c. This month
    d. This week
    e. Yesterday
    f. Today

11. Would you be willing to try to convince your peers to begin studying about attitudinal objectives?
    a. Very willing
    b. Willing
    c. Mildly willing
    d. Mildly unwilling
    e. Unwilling
    f. Very unwilling

12. When was the last time you tried to talk someone into writing their affective goals behaviorally?
    a. Never
    b. This year
    c. This month
    d. This week
    e. In the last few days
    f. Today or yesterday

13. How many times in the last year have you discussed educational accountability with another person?
    a. I never have
    b. Maybe once a year
    c. About once each month
    d. About once each week
    e. About twice each week
    f. More than twice each week

14. If *you* were given the choice about reading behavioral objectives for attitudes when would you start?
    a. Immediately
    b. Sometime within the hour
    c. Sometime today
    d. Whenever I got around to it
    e. Only when it became absolutely necessary
    f. Never

15. I've already attempted to write some affective objectives.
    a. Never
    b. Once
    c. Twice
    d. Three times
    e. Four or five times
    f. More than five times

16. Would you be willing to actively support a teachers' committee which was seeking ways to attain educational accountability?
    a. Very willing
    b. Willing
    c. Mildly willing
    d. Mildly unwilling
    e. Unwilling
    f. Very unwilling

17. When other people have mentioned books or articles which discuss the teaching of values or attitudes, how have you reacted?
    a. I've been negative
    b. I've listened—but with limited interest
    c. I've listened and been interested—but I've never read any
    d. I've listened—and read a few when I had time
    e. I've listened—and read a few within a few days
    f. I've read several right away

18. Would you be willing to lead a panel discussion with people who have already written their attitudinal goals in behavioral terms?
    a. Very willing
    b. Willing
    c. Mildly willing
    d. Mildly unwilling
    e. Unwilling
    f. Very unwilling

19. In the last four days about how much of your leisure reading has been devoted to the topic of educational accountability?
    a. None of it   d. 20–30%
    b. Less than 10%   e. 30–50%
    c. 10–20%   f. 50–100%

20. I'm so enthusiastic about learning to write affective objectives that I'd be willing to use some of my leisure time.
    a. Right now   d. In a few weeks
    b. Tomorrow   e. Some time this year
    c. In a few days   f. Never

21. I have expended the time necessary to write attitudinal objectives.
    a. Never   d. Willingly—but only mildly
    b. Unwillingly   so
    c. Unwillingly—but only e. Willingly
       mildly so   f. Very willingly

22. I would be willing to try to convince my principal to institute attitudinal accountability in our school.
    a. Very willing   d. Mildly unwilling
    b. Willing   e. Unwilling
    c. Mildly willing   f. Very unwilling

23. How many times in the last month have you tried to talk others into studying affective objectives?
    a. Never   d. 3–4 times
    b. Once   e. 5–6 times
    c. Twice   f. More than 6 times

24. I'd be willing to try to talk others into writing affective objectives.
    a. Very willing   d. Mildly unwilling
    b. Willing   e. Unwilling
    c. Mildly willing   f. Very unwilling

Make sure that you circled only *one* answer for each of the 24 items. Read page 1 now.

Pretest Answer Sheet

Fill in the lines above. Do not put your name on this sheet.

Do Not Mark in This Area

_____ a)
_____ b)   _____ n)
_____ c)   _____ s)
_____ d)
_____ e)   _____ p)
_____ f)   _____ v)
_____ g)
_____ h)   _____ t)
_____ j)   _____ q)
_____ k)
_____ l)   _____ r)   _____ u)

1. a b c d e f   13. a b c d e f
2. a b c d e f   14. a b c d e f
3. a b c d e f   15. a b c d e f
4. a b c d e f   16. a b c d e f
5. a b c d e f   17. a b c d e f
6. a b c d e f   18. a b c d e f
7. a b c d e f   19. a b c d e f
8. a b c d e f   20. a b c d e f
9. a b c d e f   21. a b c d e f
10. a b c d e f   22. a b c d e f
11. a b c d e f   23. a b c d e f
12. a b c d e f   24. a b c d e f

Make sure that you have only one answer for each of the 24 items.

RETAIN THIS SHEET

When you have finished, review page viii and begin to work through the text.

Chapter 1

Attitudes

In education it has become quite fashionable to discuss the affective domain. If you are new to the field of education and have listened to veteran teachers carry on such a discussion you probably became confused. Quite often you would hear the affective domain discussed using words like *attitudes, values, beliefs,* and *feelings.* If you listened carefully you might hear people using those words to describe what appears to be the same things.

> Tom has a bad *attitude* toward himself.
> Yet he *values* his athletic skill.
> Could it be that he *feels* inferior academically?
> I wonder if he *believes* himself a failure in school?

Are all of those words a part of the affective domain? Do they all mean the same thing? If you "value" and "feel" are you exhibiting similar or different characteristics? If you *feel* hungry is that indicative of your values? Describing the affective domain is not too difficult if you have a dictionary. Attempting to plan for, teach, and assess affect is, on the other hand, a very "sticky" business.

Should teachers attempt to teach attitudes, values, beliefs? Do you have the right, responsibility, or the privilege to teach affective behavior? Many teachers are quite sure that the affective domain is the responsibility of the home and the church. Is their certainty right or wrong? The affective domain has been the focus of many long and heated discussions in education. Many of you are aware that inclusion of sex education in the curriculum has not been attacked on the grounds that the content was inconsistent with current scientific knowledge. Rather, sex education is generally being attacked on the grounds that attitudes and beliefs were being changed. Is that argument logically sound? Do teachers really affect the affective behavior of their students?

Apparently, affective behavior is important to the community and to the schools. The latter case is the reason why this text was written. In the first chapter of this book you should become more consistent in defining affective behavior.

Attitudes, values, and beliefs are nebulous characteristics of an individual. They seem to be hidden deep within each of us. How can we hope to discuss them, to plan to foster them, or to assess them? How do we detect them in others or in ourselves? In the following pages you should gain some answers to all of the questions posed for you here.

Behavioral objectives:

A.   The student will choose appropriate synonyms for the word attitude.

B.   The student will select from a list of multiple choice items a method for assessing attitudes.

C.   The student will select from several alternatives the statements that provide the most appropriate matching rationale for the assessment of attitudes and attitudinal change.

D.   The student will state the two selected categories of human behavior that make up affective behavior.

E.   The student will state two categorical levels of any attitude.

―――

1.   An attitude is the way someone feels about something. If it is a fairly strong attitude people often say it is a belief. In other words. a belief or feeling is synonymous with an _____.

―――

attitude

2.   An attitude usually indicates that a person values something. If you value athletics you should probably be viewed by a physical education teacher as having a (good, bad) attitude towards sports.

―――

good

3.   Some words that are used to describe an attitude are feelings, beliefs, or v_____.

―――

values

4. If you jogged two miles every day, swam 20 laps three times a week, and played volleyball twice a week, a physical education teacher would think your attitude indicated a belief in the _____ of exercise.

●—

value

5. Your spouse, on the other hand, might see your athletic behavior as indicating a (bad, good) attitude toward your marriage.

●—

bad

6. You might swear great love for your spouse. But there may be some doubt in your spouse's mind about your attitude towards marriage due to your athletic _____.

●—

behavior (or a synonym)

7. The strength or existence of an attitude is often inferred from a person's _____.

●—

behavior

8. If an attitude can be inferred from someone's behavior then surely your behavior indicates something about your attitudes and _____.

●—

values

9. As soon as you walk through the door of a classroom you begin exhibiting values. If you dress neatly, your hands and face are clean, and your hair is combed one could infer that you value your personal appearance. If you smile a great deal and frown only occasionally one could then infer that you value the friendship of your pupils. Even your presence in the room would indicate that you probably value your education, money, and/or having a job. There can be no doubt. Whenever and wherever people go their behavior indicates their _____.

---

values (or needs, beliefs, attitudes, prejudices, biases, feelings)

10. Children learn to talk by listening to those around them. They learn whether they ought play with trucks or dolls from those around them. Attitudes about Christmas, taxes, blacks, policemen, sex and even mundane things like math, typing, reading and art are influenced by those around them. Children learn knowledge, skills, and _____ from those around them.

---

attitudes (or see the synonyms in the answer above)

11. Two ideas were expressed in the preceding frames. (1) Teachers exhibit values. (2) Children learn values from those around them. Using those two ideas it seems very logical to assume that school children _____
_____.

---

learn values from teachers (The exact words in your answer are not important but the idea should be exactly the same.)

12. It is pompous to believe that children learn values only from teachers. During the prepuberty years the majority of values and attitudes tend to be learned in the home. During pubescence and adolescence the peer group has a large impact on the growth of values and attitudes. By adult life our work environment and peers

influence those patterns. But _____ do influence the development of many of their pupils' _____.

━━━

teachers; attitudes

13. Teachers influence their students' attitudes in various ways. Some famous people have indicated that one or more teachers had dramatic *positive* impacts on their lives. You well know that some teachers may have had dramatic *negative* effects on your life. Teachers seem to have varying _____ on their pupils' attitudes.

━━━

effects

14. If you're teaching: What effect do you have on the attitudes of your students?
     If you're planning to teach: What effect do you hope to have on the attitudes of your students?
     Notice that both questions don't ask, "Do you have an effect?" but ask, "What kind of an _____ _____ on your students' attitudes?"

━━━

effect do you have

15. Like it or not, classroom teachers teach _____ and _____.

━━━

values; attitudes. (In either order.)

16. (a) Attitudes and values can be inferred from behavior with a fair degree of accuracy.
     (b) Pupils learn some attitudes and values from teachers.
     (c) You want to become more effective at teaching appropriate attitudes and values.

If the above assumptions are valid then we have a set of reasons for attempting to learn how to state and assess _____ objectives.

━━━

affective or attitudinal

17. First, let's make a distinction between two important words—values and attitudes. When you learned to write cognitive objectives you were writing goals for children's mental development. When you learn (as you are) to write affective objectives you will be writing goal statements for children's emotional development. Two categories make up affective or emotional goals. Those two categories are v_____ and a_____.

━━━

values; attitudes

18. Values usually deal with questions like:

   What is beauty?
   What is truth?
   What is goodness?

Values tend to be learned and held by groups. Americans are expected to value free enterprise and competition. Russians are expected to value socialism and cooperation. Those values are learned and held by many in each of those _____.

━━━

groups, societies, cultures

19. Attitudes tend to be more personalized than values. You may like hard rock music and everyone else in your family acquires a headache at the first sound. Though attitudes and values are both learned, attitudes are usually learned informally—"I think Brooks Robinson is great"—while values are usually learned formally—"I pledge allegiance to the flag . . ." Values are often capable of being stated verbally in a rational form—"I believe that God exists for

the following reasons . . ." Attitudes are often only reactions of an emotional nature—"Yuk!" (to anchovy pizza).

Match the words in the left column to the words in the right column. You may use the left column words more than once.

attitude   _____ formal
value   _____ beliefs
affect   _____ incorporates the other two
                         _____ emotional
                         _____ feelings
                         _____ rational
                         _____ informal

<u>value</u>   —formal—tend to be learned as a result of the culture
<u>value</u>   —beliefs—tend to be stated formally
<u>affective</u>—(see frame 17)
<u>attitude</u> —emotional
<u>attitude</u> —feelings—stated without any specific logic
<u>value</u>   —rational—formal logic used in stating a value
<u>attitude</u> —informal—not usually learned as a result of the culture

Don't be too concerned about differentiating between attitudes and values until you get into a philosophy class. If you understand that they're different that will be sufficient for the purposes of this program.

20. If you didn't check any books out of the library, did not subscribe to a newspaper, and said that you disliked reading an observer could be fairly certain that you had a negative attitude toward

_____.

---

reading

21. The conclusion that you had a negative attitude toward reading would be due to your observed _____.

---

behavior

22. The degree to which an attitude is held is related to your behavior. If you read Shakespeare every night your behavior would indicate that you had a (negative, positive) attitude toward Elizabethan plays.

positive

23. Your attitude is inferred from your behavior. There is no other way to measure or assess _____.

attitudes

24. Because you have already read, studied and/or written some behavioral objectives you know that there are many behaviors. One behavior is speaking. If someone tells you that they like Shakespeare's plays you have already begun to a_____ or measure their attitudes.

assess

25. Which of the following behaviors would indicate the most positive attitude towards Shakespeare's writing?
    a. Reading Shakespeare every night.
    b. Saying that you would like to read Shakespeare every night.

    a. Reading Shakespeare every night

26. The reason that reading Shakespeare every night represents a more positive attitude is that most of us are willing to say that we will do something regularly but we don't. The person who does that reading every night looks upon Shakespeare with great v_____.

value

27. Stating that you would be willing to do something and actually doing the thing represent two levels of an attitude. Though both are behaviors, they represent attitudes of two different l_____.

---

levels

28. Stating that you would be willing to live in Australia is much different than stating that you have already moved there. The first behavior indicates a more *passive* interest in Australia while the latter indicates a more _____ interest.

---

active

29. If you have already given $100 to the Salvation Army, that indicates an active interest in the organization. Merely stating that you would be willing to give $100 indicates a _____ _____.

---

passive interest

30. If you were completely inactive you neither gave $100 nor said that you would give $100. I could then infer that you probably had a n_____ attitude toward the Salvation Army.

---

negative (Assuming that you had $100 to give to anyone.)

31. Match the words in the left column to those in the right column by drawing lines.

inactive	most positive
passive	positive
active	negative

---

inactive   most positive
passive   positive
active   negative

32. All the words in the left column describe types of b_____
    while those in the right column represent types of a_____.

---

    behaviors; attitudes

33. The type of behavior a person uses in relation to something indicates the d_____ of his attitude toward that thing.

---

    degree

34. The more active the behavior the more p_____ the attitude, generally.

---

    positive

35. Someone might say that they would be willing to try flying an airplane but a more positive attitude toward airplane flying would be indicated if they said that they had already tried _____
    _____   _____.

---

    flying an airplane

36. Stating that you have already done something is usually an indication of a *more* positive attitude. Stating that you would be willing to try something is an indication of a _____ positive attitude.

---

    less

37. Now that you are about to finish this section of the program you should be able to discuss the following concepts:

   a. attitude
   b. attitudinal levels
   c. reasons for attitudinal objectives
   d. reasons for attitudinal assessment

Once you're sure that you understand those concepts go on to Chapter 2.

Affective Categories

As you learned in the previous chapter there are at least two levels to an attitude—passive and active. Intuitively, however, we all know that there is more to types of attitudes than just that. Witness the following conversation which is similar to those most of us have experienced at one time or another:

Him: I love you.

Her: You always say that—but you don't mean it.

Him: Of course I do. Why would you say I don't?

Her: You never have gone to meet my parents.

Him: Oh that again. You know I'm busy now. That doesn't mean that I don't love you.

Her: Okay, when was the last time you bought me a present?

Him: Last week. I bought you a ticket to that concert.

Her: Big deal, you cheapskate! Why didn't you go with me?

Him: That's the night I bowl. I love you dearly, but I was bowling long before I met you—and you knew I bowled when I met you.

Her: Some love! When was the last time you told someone else you loved *me*—like your dead-beat brother!

Him: Now watch it! Besides, he doesn't even live here anymore.

Her: So our love is a secret?

Him: Don't be silly. Do you want me to shout out my love from the highest mountain?

Her: No. But would you be willing to give up smoking for the rest of your life—just for me?

Him: Come on now! I already said I love you!

Her: See! You always *say* that!

Ah, the trials and tribulations of love even fit the affective domain. She called him a hypocrite because his behavior was inconsistent with his verbalizations. By asking for examples of his behavior she actually was trying to assess the degree of love he actually felt. Did you notice how she constantly escalated her argument? Eventually, she placed him in a position of demonstrating his love by giving up another love— smoking. (Only a smoker can empathize with the agony such a decision would cause.) When people use phrases like "their love is of great depth" they are intimating that they can quantify the level of love the couple demonstrates. Apparently, all of us know, at least intuitively, that certain behaviors can be used to infer what degree of attitude exists. But what are those behaviors? What words describe those behaviors succinctly? Can you organize behaviors to infer the degree of someone's attitude?

In education, as in love, the quantification of a person's attitude is of interest. Just as in love, the techniques involved in the quantification process in education is a difficult matter. One of the most widely used procedures is that of scaling. If properly done, scaling provides items to which most people can agree, some items to which about half the people will agree, and a few items to which a few people will agree. Attitude scales, then, provide a set of items which should allow all people to represent their attitudes accurately. Scores from such scales are used to compare one person's attitude with another's.

Constructing an attitude scale is a long and arduous procedure. Some scales with high validity and high reliability have taken years to construct. Obviously, classroom teachers don't have the time to devote to such activities. If a teacher wants to assess very specific attitudes he usually is unable to find a scale that meets his needs. A classroom teacher is caught in an uncomfortable position. If he wants to be able to compare student attitudes he may be forced to choose between spending years constructing a useful instrument or using one that is available but not aligned with his assessment needs.

To overcome that problem researchers have attempted to develop categorization schemes which will allow teachers and test designers to match their items and objectives to specific attitudinal benchmarks. The assumption underlying each of those schemes is that it is possible to identify the level or amount of attitudinal commitment which any person holds. The outcome of those schemes is supposed to be an attitudinal scale that will allow researchers and teachers to compare attitudes of vastly different people.

The pattern for categorizing attitudes that you will be taught in the next chapter is admittedly crude. It has, however, seemed to work when used with children and adults. Until a better scheme is devised the pattern you'll now learn seems to be the most useful for classroom teachers.

Behavioral objectives:

A. The student will list the attitudinal stages sequentially.

B. The student will match attitudinal statements to their appropriate stage and level.

Go on to the next frame.

●━━━━━━━━━━━━━━━━━━━━━━━━━━━━━━━━━━━━━━━●

38. Indicating that you would be willing to do something and actually doing it, though different levels, are both representative of positive attitudes. Stating that you would be unwilling to try something and stating that you have not tried something would represent a _____ _____.

●━━━━━━━━━━━━━━━━━━━━━━━━━━━━━━━━━━━━━━━●

negative attitude

39. There are two ways of stating a willingness to do something. For example, person A might state that he would be willing to spend three hours learning about microbiology; person B might state that he would rather spend three hours studying microbiology *rather than watching his favorite movie* on TV. Person A would have agreed that studying microbiology was interesting. Person B stated that it was so interesting that he was willing to give up something to pursue his choice. Person B demonstrated a more _____ _____ toward microbiology.

●━━━━━━━━━━━━━━━━━━━━━━━━━━━━━━━━━━━━━━━●

positive attitude

40. Imagine that person A agreed with the first of the following questions while person B agreed with the second. Which person exhibited the most positive attitude toward archaeology?

A agrees: I would be willing to spend my vacation studying archaeology.

B agrees: I would be willing to study archaeology.

●━━━━━━━━━━━━━━━━━━━━━━━━━━━━━━━━━━━━━━━●

A did—because he chose to spend a specific time studying. That requires more commitment than just saying he would be willing to study archeology—sometime.

41. Which of the following represents the most positive attitude towards mountain climbing? (Circle A or B)

    A agrees: I would be willing to try mountain climbing rather than go to Europe.

    B agrees: I have tried mountain climbing rather than go to Europe.

B did. If you didn't get that one correct then you're not paying attention.

42. We now have our four categories of behavior which might be used in assessing someone's attitude. The four behaviors are listed below. On the line in front of each behavior number them from 1 to 4. The number 1 will represent the *least* positive indication while the number 4 the *most* positive indication of an attitude.

    _____ A. Expression of a willingness to choose between two things of value to the subject.
    _____ B. An indication that something has been tried.
    _____ C. Expression of a willingness to try something.
    _____ D. An indication that a choice has been made between two things of value to the subject.

A—3; B—2; C—1; D—4 (Reexamine frames 39–41 if you categorized those incorrectly.)

43. The first two levels are called the Experiment stage. In the Experiment stage the first level is the passive level of stating that you would be willing to _____ _____. The second level is the _____ level of stating that you have already tried something.

try something; active

44. The third and fourth levels comprise the Choice stage. In the Choice stage, the first level is the p_____ level of stating that you would be willing to make a _____ between the object and something else of value. The second level involves stating that you _____ _____ _____ _____ _____ .

●━●

passive
choice
have already made a choice

45. The following summary may help you to remember the type of attitude, the behavior, and the stages.

   I Experiment stage
      A. Expression of a willingness to try something (passive)
      B. Indication that something has been tried (active)

   II Choice stage
      A. Expression of a choice between the attitudinal object and something else of value (passive)
      B. Indication that choices have been made (active)

   Now, without looking back, the first stage is _____ and the second is _____ .

●━●

Oh, come on now! Look them up yourself!

46. The active levels denoted as Experiment and Choice may be measured by other than oral behavioral data. If a student checks out a book from the library obviously he is actively involved in reading. When presented the choice of going home or going to the library to check out a book, the student's physical rather than verbal _____ can be measured at the _____ stage.

●━●

behavior; choice

47. On the line in front of each of the following statements place a number that represents the degree of positiveness which each statement possesses. Number the least positive 1 and the most positive 3.

     _____A. I have used my leisure time to paint.
     _____B. I would be willing to join an oil painting club where we discussed each other's work critically.
     _____C. I would be willing to try oil painting.

━━━

A—2; B—3; C—1
Painting oils by yourself does not require quite as much commitment to that art form as does regularly discussing with and having your work criticized by others.

48. If you're thinking ahead you may have guessed one or two things. We are now beginning to discuss another stage—and the level alluded to above, 47B, is the passive level. The active level in this stage would require someone to state that they have a_____ shared an a_____ with other enthusiasts.

━━━

already
activity

49. Does statement A or B represent the active level in the third stage?

A. I have participated in several meetings of the Art Critics Association.

B. I would be willing to sign a petition demanding presidential recognition of the Art Critics Association.

━━━

A is the active level. The subject has already demonstrated his attitude behaviorally. In B the subject is known only to *believe* himself ready to act—which may or may not come about.

50. The third stage is called the Concurrence stage. In its first level the subject can express a w_____ to concur and actively participate with other enthusiasts. In its second level the subject can i_____ that he has already c_____ with other enthusiasts.

willingness; indicate; concurred

51. Concurrence, either in the active or passive state, can be measured objectively if a test item requires a specific behavioral manifestation or active participation. When the subject is asked about his willingness to participate he may respond positively. But in his mind participation may mean attendance as a peripheral figure. Therefore, passive concurrence items need to ask questions concerning a willingness to lead or to _____ participate. Active concurrence items need to ask questions about whether the person has already l_____ or actively _____ _____ a _____ of other interested persons.

actively; led; participated with a group

52. Fill in the blanks for the listing below for the third stage.

III _____ stage
   A. Expression of a willingness to share an _____
   _____ _____ _____.
   B. Indication that a certain type of behavior has been actively _____ with other enthusiasts.

Concurrence; activity with other enthusiasts; shared

53. Order the following statements from 1 to 4. The number 1 will identify the *least* positive indication of an attitude. The number 4 will be the *most* positive.

_____A. Several times I have chosen to jog rather than watch TV.

_____B. I would be willing to give up dinner to jog.

_____C. I would be willing to try jogging.

_____D. Several times I have chaired meetings where we discussed the benefits of jogging.

●-●

A—3; B—2 (As soon as you do give up dinner then I'll *really* believe you.); C—1; D—4

54. Sharing an activity, either passively or actively, with other enthusiasts is something most of us have done. Attendance at church, football games, and movies in theaters indicates a certain degree of favorableness towards an object. But attempting to involve others in an activity is to proselyte. Can you guess what the next stage is called? Write it on this line. _____ How many levels do you think that stage has? _____

●-●●-●-●-●-●-●-●-●-●-●-●

Proselyte; 2—active and passive

55. Finish the following two statements:

A. I would be _____ to go door-to-door to encourage others to vote for the school levy.

B. I have gone door-to-door to _____ _____

_____ _____ _____ _____

_____ _____.

●-●

willing; encourage others to vote for the school levy

56. Statement _____ above was the active statement while _____ was the passive statement.

B; A

57. The reason that the Proselyte stage requires a more favorable attitude than Concurrence is that the latter only requires the subject to interact with other _____. The Proselyte stage requires that the subject try to get others to _____ themselves.

enthusiasts; involve

58. Read the following statement:

I would be willing to act as a panel member when our Veterans' club discusses veterans' benefits.

That is a passive Concurrence item, right? (Right!) On the following lines, first change it to a passive proselyte item, then second, change it to an active Proselyte statement.

A _____

_____

B _____

_____

Your answers will vary from these below in the words used but the intent should be the same.

A. I would be willing to act as a panel member when our Veterans' club requests more veterans' aid from Congress.

B. I have been a panel member when our Veterans' club requested more veterans' aid from the legislature.

Neither Congress nor a state legislature could be categorically defined as enthusiasts of veterans' affairs—though members of a Veterans' club could be.

59. Match the statements in the left column to those in the right.

Stage and Level		Statement
A. Experiment—passive	____ (1)	I have attended an Alcoholics Anonymous club meeting.
B. Experiment—active		
C. Choice—passive	____ (2)	I have spoken to civic clubs trying to get them to donate funds to Alcoholics Anonymous.
D. Choice—active		
E. Concurrence—passive		
F. Concurrence—active	____ (3)	I have been a speaker at Alcoholics Anonymous club meetings.
G. Proselyte—passive		
H. Proselyte—active	____ (4)	I would be happy to attend an Alcoholics Anonymous meeting with a member of the club.

••

(1)- B—see frames 39–43 if you missed that one.

(2)—H—see frames 54–57 if you missed that one.

(3)—F—see frames 48–52 if you missed that one.

(4)—A—that one was tricky. Attendance with a member does not mean any involvement occurred (see frame 54). Little commitment was necessary to Alcoholics Anonymous. Many people attend different types of churches and don't experience or expect to experience any new-found commitments. They just want to try or experiment with a new activity.

60. Patrick Henry once said, "Give me liberty or give me death." Certainly he expressed a highly positive attitude toward liberty. On the other hand, Nathan Hale's statement, "I regret that I have but one life to give for my country," was made in a setting where his statement was even more positive. Henry's statement represents a p____ attitude toward liberty. Hale's willingness to sacrifice his own life was an ____ representation of his attitude.

••

passive; active

61. Both men were willing to make the ultimate sacrifice—at least Patrick Henry said he was. I bet you can't name the next stage? _____ (I'm sure you know why it's the last stage though.)

•••

Sacrifice stage

62. How many levels do you anticipate are in the Sacrifice stage?

_____

•••

two—passive and active

63. Label the following statements, which exemplify the Sacrifice stage, as either passive or active.

_____ A. I attended your wedding rather than compete in the finals of the Olympics.
_____ B. I am willing to give up my career to raise your children.

•••

A—active; B—passive

64. One must be careful not to confuse the Sacrifice stage with the _____ stage.

•••

Choice—see the next frame if you're confused. If you're sure that you understand the difference between Choice and Sacrifice stages skip frame 65 and begin with frame 66.

65. The major distinction between the Choice and Sacrifice stages is that in the Choice stage you can easily go back to or reacquire the object which you did not choose. In the Sacrifice stage the unchosen object is lost or only retrievable through great difficulty. To ensure that you understand match the following:

A. Choice—passive
B. Choice—active
C. Sacrifice—passive
D. Sacrifice—active

_____ (1) I sold my classic 1929 Stutz Bearcat to make a down payment on our house.

_____ (2) I'm willing to give up my poker night to attend my daughter's wedding.

_____ (3) I'm willing to be sterilized prior to marriage to aid in combating the population explosion.

_____ (4) I have served as a chaperone at a YMCA dance rather than go camping.

●●●

(1) D
(2) A
(3) C
(4) B

66. Money should not be used as the "Other" valued item or object for Sacrifice items unless that money was used to purchase an object at the expense of another irretrievable object. Three examples of times when money can be used in the Sacrifice stage are shown below:

I would be willing to spend the money necessary to clean up the environment rather than
(pay for my daughter's wedding.)
(give my wife a large funeral.)
(send my only child to college.)

For Sacrifice items money should be used as an object only in situations similar to those above.

Go on to the next frame.

●●●

67. Match the following five statements with the stage and level:

A. Experiment—passive
B. Experiment—active
C. Choice—passive
D. Choice—active
E. Concurrence—passive
F. Concurrence—active
G. Proselyte—passive
H. Proselyte—active
I. Sacrifice—passive
J. Sacrifice—active

_____ (1) I'm willing to ask others to work on the school paper.

_____ (2) I gave up an athletic scholarship to work on the school paper.

_____ (3) I've worked on the school paper previously.

_____ (4) I use my spare time to work on the school paper.

_____ (5) I would enjoy leading a meeting to discuss common problems with others who work on the school paper.

* * *

(1) G; (2) J; (3) B; (4) D; (5) E

Do not go on unless you understand why the above answers were correct. Go back and reread the appropriate sections if you don't understand. From here on it will be imperative that you comprehend the five stages.

68. Now that you understand the relationship of the five stages and of the two levels there are some problems with the category system we have been using.

A. You must be very careful when you write or discuss objectives or items. It is very easy to think that you have described a proselyte situation when it is a concurrence situation or to confuse sacrifice and choice. You must be sure that you understand the definition for each stage.

B. The distance between the experimental active level and the choice active level cannot be assumed to be the same distance as that between the choice active level and the concurrence active level. The category system is not assumed to be a ratio scale but one made up of units of variable length—an ordinal scale. Operation with data that you might collect, such as adding or subtracting, are done with the user's discretion.

C.   This category system works quite well for many situations. Some situations, however, don't seem to fit well under the scheme. For most objectives you would want to write for affective school goals this pattern will work well.

D.   There is a logical trap into which you may fall when you analyze the attitudinal hierarchy we've discussed. It seems that the choice stage requires more commitment than the experiment stage $(Ch > E)$ and that the active level requires more commitment than the passive level $(A > P)$. Therefore, it would seem that the following pattern ought to be true: $ChA > ChP$ $EA > EP$. Whether that pattern exists in the attitudes of people generally is certainly only speculative. The pattern is to be considered useful in thinking about the attitudes of people—but not a pattern that exists for all people in all situations.*

---

69.   Now that you understand the categorization pattern you should be able to meet the objectives which were listed at the beginning of this chapter. If you are unable to (1) list the stages and/or levels sequentially or (2) match objectives to those levels and/or stages, then reread these sections. If you're sure that you can meet those objectives then go on to Chapter 3 where you will learn how to state attitudinal objectives.

---

* The results of some unpublished pilot work examining the above hierarchy have provided support for two conclusions. First, passive level questions generate higher scores than active level questions, i.e., subjects respond more positively to items requiring less commitment. Second, items at the active level that are of common experience generate higher scores than those of uncommon experience: e.g., two items at the same stage, at the active level and written for the same construct, will not generate similar scores unless the behaviors in question are similar in degree of commonality in the subject's life.

Chapter 3

Stating Affective Objectives

Readers who have previously learned about stating cognitive behavioral objectives will find the content of this chapter somewhat familiar. Because cognitive and affective objectives are designed to be clear-cut statements of purpose, there is a similarity in writing style. You'll not, it is hoped, be unduly burdened, however, by redundancy. Because the topics which are the focus for cognitive and affective objectives differ there will be new ideas to consider in this chapter. A few of those ideas are identified in the next four paragraphs.

You may have wondered about the sources of affective behavioral objectives. From what set of references can they be efficiently and effectively drawn? The next chapter should help answer that.

There are some fairly well defined procedures to use in stating affective objectives. Procedures that you can use to check your own objectives will be stated shortly.

Certainly you will need a chance to try your hand at writing objectives for specific topics. If this program meets your learning needs you will become noticeably more proficient at stating clearly your attitudinal objectives. Practice activities make up later sections of this chapter.

If you are still a bit shaky in using or identifying stages and levels, the next chapter will reinforce your retention of those taxonomies by asking you to employ them as you write affective objectives. You'll be taught to write objectives which can be categorized by level and stage.

That may sound like a very rigorous set of tasks. Actually, it sounds much more difficult than it will really be for you. Most readers have found this chapter to be one that requires attention but not an excessive mental effort. In other words, have faith. You'll learn to do all of those things with your usual style and grace.

Behavioral objectives:

A. The student will demonstrate his knowledge of the interrelationship of the two hierarchies by writing three objectives appropriate for a given level and stage.

B. The student will correctly order the steps in planning for, teaching, and assessing affective objectives.

C. The student will be able to write attitudinal objectives that include all four components.

Go on to the next frame.

━━

70. In Chapter 1 we said that many values and attitudes that children learn are acquired in school. Therefore, it is imperative that we as teachers focus our attention on the attitudes and _____ we _____.

━━

values; teach

71. To ensure that we teach attitudes acceptable to ourselves and to the community several things should occur. *First,* we should choose those affective g_____ that we believe we would like to teach or reinforce.

━━

goals. (One goal might be "a better attitude toward math.")

72. *Second,* once those attitudinal goals are chosen we should state them as o_____ for ourselves and our students.

━━

objectives. (Objectives are more specific than goals. An objective for the goal in frame 72 might be "The students will indicate an improved attitude toward math by checking more books out of the library which are biographies of mathematicians.")

73. Once the objective(s) (is, are) stated then, *third,* it is necessary to try to determine how one might teach those attitudes. Many authors have discussed the teaching of values and attitudes. This program is not designed to meet that goal. However, a small bibliography of readings is provided at the end of the program which may be of some use.

Go on to the next frame.

●──●

74. The *fourth* step is that of determining the success of our teaching of affective goals. The assessment of the students' _____ will indicate whether the _____ was met.

●──●

attitudes; objective

75. A final step is called revising the teaching plan—and it occurs, obviously, after you've taught the lesson. The reason for including a step on revision is that once you have determined whether you were successful in obtaining your objectives you can decide about the effectiveness of your teaching and possibly the validity of your choice of objective. The step following the four of (1) selecting a value or attitude, (2) stating an objective, (3) selecting the learning activities, and (4) assessing the attainment of the objective is (5) _____ the _____ and/or the _____.

●──●

revising; procedures; objective

76. There are five steps in preparing and teaching either affective or cognitive objectives. Those steps are listed below. On the line in front of each step number them from 1 to 5. The first step will be the first thing you should do in preparing to teach.

_____A. Selecting the learning activities
_____B. Stating an objective
_____C. Assessing the degree of attainment of the objective
_____D. Revising the procedure or the objective(s)
_____E. Selecting a set (may be one) of values or attitudes to teach.

●──●

A—3; B—2; C—4; D—5; E—1 (Reread frames 70–75 if you missed *any* of these.)

77. The remainder of this program will teach you how to accomplish really only two of those tasks—stating affective objectives and assessing those objectives. Selecting the goals is a matter of your choice and that of your community. Planning to teach and actually teaching for affect is a topic that encompasses all of education and is an impossible topic to adequately discuss in one source such as this. Because revising your plans encompasses the steps just mentioned we'll discuss that one only briefly later in the program. From this point, however, this program will emphasize two steps. They are: (1) _____ and (2) _____.

---

(1)   Stating affective objectives; and
(2)   Assessing affective objectives

78. Let's assume that the pattern for categorizing objectives which we discussed in Chapter 2 is cumulative. If a person agrees with statements at the Choice stage it can be assumed that he would agree also with items at the _____ stage.

Experiment

79. Though we assume the pattern is cumulative, in reality it may not be, i.e., just because I said I was willing to make a choice does not mean that I have already experimented. That is just an assumption this program is organized around. If a person agrees with items at the Concurrence stage he is assumed to agree with those at the _____ and _____ stages.

Choice; Experiment (In either order)

80. If you'll remember the above assumption it may help to clarify your thinking as you learn to write objectives. When writing objectives you must indicate what behavior the student will manifest. In writing attitudinal objectives you must identify the stage to which students are expected to agree. An example is shown below:

At the completion of the course of study, 90% of the students will state that they have checked out one Shakespearian play from the library. Such action will occur as a result of their choice and not a teacher-directed assignment.

The above objective would be classified at the _____ stage and the _____ level.

● ●

Choice; second or active

81. The objective assumed that the student would also state that he was _____ to read Shakespeare if given a choice.

● ●

willing

82. Complete the following objective for the first level of the Concurrence stage.

Upon completion of the programmed materials, 80% of the students will state a _____ to _____ with other participants about writing affective objectives.

● ●

willingness; discuss or interact or speak

83. On the following lines write an attitudinal objective for a series of lectures on pollution. State the objective in such a manner that three-fourths of the participants will reach the second level of the Proselyte stage.

_____

_____

_____

● ●

Two weeks after attending the lecture series on pollution, 75% of the participants will state that they have attempted to involve others in the battle against pollution.

Your objective may vary somewhat from the one above. Except for some words in the above objective yours should be quite similar to the suggested answer.

84. The behavior required in these attitudinal objectives has been to _____ a willingness to be involved or an indication that involvement has occurred.

---

state

85. Though it makes it easier to write objectives when the behavior is always "state," a difficulty exists. Subjects may not be honest in their agreement or disagreement with a statement. The best way to allow subjects to be _____ is to allow them to be anonymous.

---

honest

86. That means it is very difficult to measure a specific *individual's* progress (or regress) attitudinally unless you observe his behavior via other means. With the method in this program you can gain some knowledge, though, of a _____ attitude.

---

group's or class's

87. Complete the following objectives that deal with attitudes toward dancing. Upon completion of 10 lessons:

   A. 90% of the students will _____ that they would be _____ to dance at a party.
   B. 80% of the _____ will _____ that they have _____ at a party.
   C. 70% of the _____ will _____ _____ _____ would be _____ to

_____ at a party rather than just talk with their friends.

D. 60% of the _____ will _____

_____ have _____ at a

_____

_____

_____.

• •

A. state; willing
B. students; state; danced
C. students; state that they; willing; dance
D. students; state that they; danced; party rather than just talk with their friends.

88. Two differences exist in the objectives on dancing. First, each succeeding objective required a higher level commitment toward _____. Second, each succeeding objective had a lower _____ _____ value.

• •

dancing; percentage

89. Because more commitment was required (more, fewer) students could be expected to meet each succeeding objective.

• •

fewer

90. You would expect (many, few) students to state that they had tried jogging. You would expect (more, fewer) to say that they would be willing to attend civic club meetings where they would be individually responsible for requesting a donation for the construction of a jogging track in the park.

• •

many; fewer

91. The rule is, then, the (lesser, greater) the commitment the (lesser, greater) the number of students who can realistically be expected to agree with a statement.

●-●●●

lesser; greater *or* greater; lesser

92. When writing very specific attitudinal objectives four components should be included. Those components are:

  a) Who will be the performer(s)
  b) What will be the behavior
  c) What degree of attitude will be acceptable
  d) What level and stage will be measured.

Consider the following objective:

70% of the students will state that they would be willing to dance at a party rather than just talk with their friends.

Analyze the objective to make sure that each of the three components listed below are included. Do the following:

Component   *Answer*

  a)   Underline the part that describes who will be the performer(s).
  b)   Circle the part that describes the behavior sought from the performer(s).
  c)   Put parentheses ( ) around the part that describes the degree of attitude which will be acceptable to denote that the objective has been met.

●-●●

<u>70% of the students</u> ⟨will state⟩ that they (would be willing) to dance at a party rather than just talk with their friends.

93. In the above objective it is also possible to denote the level and stage which is being measured. The word ＿＿＿＿＿＿＿ identifies the level while the words ＿＿＿＿＿＿＿＿＿＿＿＿＿

＿＿＿＿＿＿＿＿＿＿＿＿ identify the stage.

●-●●

willing—passive level
rather than just talk with their friends—choice stage

94.   Let's try one more. Construct an objective that requires that one-half of the students will indicate an active attiude toward convincing at least two other people to study marine sciences as an elective. When you've done that complete the following:

    a)   Underline the part that describes who will be the performer(s).

    b)   Circle the part that describes the behavior sought from the performer(s).

    c)   Put parentheses ( ) around the part that describes the degree of attitude which will be acceptable to denote that the objective has been met.

    d)   Put brackets [ ] around the part that describes the level and stage being assessed.

_____

_____

_____

- -

<u>50% of the students</u> (will state) that they [have attempted to convince] (two or more students) to elect the marine sciences course.

Your objective and answers can vary a bit from the one above.

95.   In the objective related to dancing you may have been confused by one point. In that objective how did the words "would be willing" indicate the degree of attitude? Read the following test item for the objective for dancing:

       Would you now be willing to dance at a party rather than just talk with your friends?

       a. Very willing   d. Mildly unwilling
       b. Willing   e. Unwilling
       c. Mildly willing   f. Very unwilling

Which of the above three answers would the students need to select to indicate a willingness to dance at a party? _____

- -

a, b, or c

96. By identifying the exact degree necessary to meet that objective you have stated very clearly what goal you have in mind for indicating a satisfactory amount of student commitment. Analyze one more objective and its corresponding test item. A suitable test item related to the marine sciences objective (frame #94) follows.

> How many other students have you attempted to convince to take the course on marine sciences?
>
> a. None   d. Three
> b. One   e. Four
> c. Two   f. Five or more

Which answers would be acceptable in the above item to indicate that a student had met the following objective? _____

> 50% of the students will state that they have attempted to convince two or more students to elect the marine science course.

---

c, d, e, or f

97. There are other ways to write objectives that are less time-consuming. For example, you may wish to write an objective for student attitudes that describe their scores on a total test rather than specific items. Such an objective follows:

> At the completion of the unit on Roman numerals the students' gain scores (post-test minus pretest) will indicate an increased growth in attitude toward studying other numeration systems.

After you have had a chance to learn how to write and score attitudinal items we'll return to stating objectives. With your knowledge about assessing attitudes you'll then be ready to learn how to state objectives more efficiently.

Go on to the next frame.

---

98. In this section you should have learned:

(1) How to order the steps in planning for, teaching, and assessing affective instruction.

(2) How to write affective objectives in behavioral terms.

(3)   How to write behavioral affective objectives specific to a stage and to a level.

(4)   How to diagnose and write objectives using four components.

If you are unsure about your ability to do that you might do well to stop and practice before continuing on to the next frame.

* * *

99.   Due to the number of concepts which have been introduced to this point you may find it to your advantage to stop work for awhile. One generalization which seems to be true of the way in which people learn is that they need time to reflect about the ideas they have acquired. To help structure your reflective process reread the objectives preceding Chapters 1–3. You should now be able to meet all of those objectives. Once you've read those objectives sit and think—or rest. You won't be lazy—just wise in the ways in which people learn.

* * *

Chapter 4

Writing Attitudinal Items

Writing attitudinal items is like teaching. Both processes involve a bit of science and a bit of art. Though the following pages may not transform you into an artistic writer you should become technically a better writer of attitudinal items. There are several reasons for anticipating an improvement in your technical skills.

You should expect to learn some generalized procedures for assessing the quality of an attitudinal scale. Those procedures will include how to use the concept of validity in assessing a scale you or another person has written; how to use the concept of the normal curve in deciding how to interpret the anticipated results; and, how to evaluate whether an item stands a chance of being understood before students ever read it. Those procedures should help you to make judgements about an attitudinal scale prior to its use.

A second reason to anticipate an improvement in your writing skill is that the factor of redundancy may be controlled. You may have noticed that many attitude scales have answer choices that are highly repetitive. There is reason to believe that due to the similarity in answers which can be chosen such an attitude scale restricts the student to a response set—only certain attitudes tend to be assessed. To overcome that possibility you will be taught a variety of ways to state the answer selections which students can choose.

Many readers do now or plan to work with students who are less than proficient readers. Those readers may be concerned that attitudinal devices are of limited worth in light of their students' skills. To alleviate that concern, the latter portion of this chapter will identify one procedure for assessing the attitudes of non-readers.

A complete analysis of the technical skills involved in writing attitudinal items surpasses the intent of this text. However, the skills you will learn here will be sufficient to get you started. When you've finished you should be able to write attitudinal items that seem capable of assessing the appropriate attitude, lacking in redundancy, and, if necessary, suitable for adaptation to use with non-readers.

Behavioral objectives:

A.   The student will apply his knowledge of each of the four selected measures (question types) by choosing from a list matching examples.

B.   The student will demonstrate his knowledge of the four selected measures by constructing appropriate examples for each.

C.   The student will employ the informal criteria for attitudinal statements by correctly identifying, when shown an item, two or more criteria that are violated.

Go on the the next frame.

----

100.   People vary in the types of addition problems they can solve. People vary in the types of paintings they like. If only one type of addition problem is tested you find out which people can work only that problem. If you ask only one question about painting you will find out very little about a person's attitude toward painting. In both cases, if several types of questions are asked you can find out which people know a great deal about addition or which people have the best attitudes toward painting. The same holds true for assessing all attitudes. A wide range of items should be used to assess the range of commitment. A person responding positively to a low level of commitment may respond negatively to items that require a high level of commitment. In other words, the more kinds of questions we ask the greater the degree of variance will be found. Eventually we should come close to identifying specifically how each individual differs from his peers in terms of attitude. What would be the best number of items to give on an attitude scale—1, 10, 100?

10—because it would provide a closer approximation of the range of attitudes than one item. One hundred items would be better except people get tired and may not finish. Not only that, they would learn to hate; do you enjoy taking a test with 100 items?

101. A recent popular expression in our country has been, "America, love it or leave it." When a political conservative used that phrase he generally meant accept the goals and actions of the nation or leave it. Other people or groups believed the phrase implied different thoughts. People responded to that single phrase differently in what they thought it meant. Going to church, atheism, voting, carrying arms, dissent were justified as indicators of "loving" America. If you asked enough people—several thousand—to answer an attitudinal item and if the question is a "good" one you should get a response pattern that looks like a _____ curve.

_____

normal or bell-shaped

102. The reason you would get a normal curve is that a few people would strongly agree, a few would strongly disagree, and the majority would be some place in the middle. If the above is true and you wrote a "good" item then the *average* response to that item would be: strongly positive, positive, neutral, negative, strongly negative.

_____

neutral (see below)

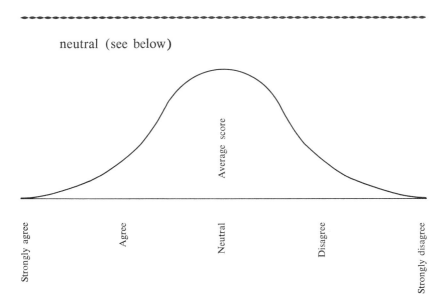

103. The problem with a neutral statement is that it tells you very little about the person. He may be ambivalent, he may not care, or he may not know what you're talking about. If you asked a class of third-graders about their attitude toward the "military-industrial complex" in the United States most of them would express a _____ attitude.

---

neutral—because, probably, most don't know what those words mean. (One problem is that they may not know what "neutral" means so they may choose a different answer.)

104. Suppose you wanted to know about a person's attitude toward Richard Burton as an actor. If you asked the question, "Do you believe Richard Burton's performance in *Cleopatra* was a good one?" a subject might choose an answer like "neutral," "I don't know," "unsure." Those answers give you (little, much) information about the respondent's attitude.

---

little. He may not: know Richard Burton; have seen *Cleopatra;* know any criteria for judging actors; or he may be saying that Burton's performance was occasionally satisfactory.

105. A _____ response is almost impossible to interpret.

---

neutral (If you got that wrong, stop! You need more rest—not more information.)

106. Because of the lack of utility of neutral answers to attitudinal items the questions you will be taught to write will not allow for neutral answers.

---

107. If you wanted to determine most accurately (validly) a person's attitude you should ask (one, several) questions.

---

several

108. Just as we assess the degree of peoples' attitudes more accurately by measuring varying levels of commitment, so should we use varying types of questions. If only one type of question is used we are measuring the subject's attitude in a restrictive setting. Psychologists commonly use four types of measures to assess behavior. By using those measures we then could use a wider variety of questions to which a subject could respond. This should make our assessment of the subject's attitude even more accurate. With this introduction then we'll begin to write attitudinal questions.

Go on to the next frame.

----

109. You may find yourself becoming very redundant as you write attitudinal questions. The following section may alleviate that. Look at the following three questions and choose the item that is not like the others. Circle the appropriate answer. (Hint: Focus on the question—not the answers.)

    A. When you read a play by Shakespeare how much time do you usually spend in one sitting?
        1) less than 15 minutes   3) about an hour
        2) about 15–30 minutes   4) well over an hour

    B. How much did you spend on your Shakespeare books?
        1) $1 or less   3) more than $5—less
        2) more than $1—less   than $10
             than $5   4) more than $10

    C. How often do you read Shakespeare's plays for recreational purposes?
        1) at least once a week   3) about once a year
        2) at least once a month   4) never

Be careful. Determine what type of question is being asked—not what attitudinal stage is being assessed.

    C is different

110. Questions A and B in the preceding frame were asking about the size of a response . . . "how much." Question C was asking about the frequency of a response. Questions A and B dealt with magnitude while C dealt with _____.

----

    frequency

111. The distinction between magnitude and frequency is sometimes difficult to understand. Magnitude deals with the size of a response at a specific point in time. For example, measures such as age, height, and _____ are measures of magnitude.

——

weight

112. Frequency is different in that we're not concerned with the size of the response—we're only concerned with how many responses occur. A succinct definition of frequency is "the rate at which responses are made during a specified time period." Which of the following is an example of a frequency measure: a) score on a typing test *or* b) amount of beer drunk by an individual?

——

(a) is the better example of a frequency measure. Frequency measures are usually turned into rate scores. For example, in a typing test the total number of words you typed is divided by the minutes you typed to get a words per minute score. (b) is a measure of how much beer you drank last night but it is not indicative of how much you'll drink this morning. A frequency score is designed to be used to predict future events—a magnitude score is used to assess how much exists now.
(Isn't that just like a teacher? The answer is longer than the question.)

113. Which kinds of measures are designed to answer each of the following questions:

(a) How often does something occur? (frequency, magnitude)
(b) How much exists now?   (frequency, magnitude)

——

(a) frequency
(b) magnitude

If you understand the difference between magnitude and frequency please skip the next two frames.

114. Let's use a different explanation to make the distinction between magnitude and frequency. Examine the following pictures of measures then answer the question that follows.

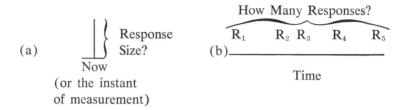

Which of the above diagrams, a or b, is a picture of magnitude?

•••

(a) is magnitude while (b) represents frequency

115. Using the above picture to aid you, identify which of the following are magnitude measures and which are frequency measures.

(a)＿＿＿＿ the amount of money you're willing to spend for a bicycle

(b)＿＿＿＿ the number of children you have

(c)＿＿＿＿ the number of times you jog each week

(d)＿＿＿＿ the number of minutes you jogged yesterday

(e)＿＿＿＿ the number of minutes you'll jog tomorrow

(f)＿＿＿＿ a batting average

(g)＿＿＿＿ the number of trips to the dentist this year

•••

(a)   magnitude—how much now

(b)   magnitude—how many now

(c)   frequency—how often or the rate at which (see frame 112 for help.)

(d)   magnitude—how many at that time

(e)   magnitude—how many at that time

(f)   frequency—how often can we expect him to hit or at what rate

(g) magnitude—how often; usually not stated as a rate. If you wanted to know if the individual went so often per month then it is a measure of frequency. If you're only interested in this year then it is a measure of magnitude.

116. Look at the following questions (minus the possible answers) and determine which one of the three is different. Circle the appropriate letter.

   A. How often per week do you jog one mile or more?
   B. If you decided that you would like to read about jogging how long would it take you to find time to go to the library and check out a book?
   C. In the last year, how often have you tried to convince others to jog?

   B is different

117. In A and C above you read questions about (magnitude, frequency). In B a question was asked about latency. Latency refers to how _____ it takes someone to respond.

   frequency
   long

118. _____ is a measure of time.

   Latency

119. Latency differs from frequency in that frequency is a measure of how many responses occurred during a time period. Responses are measured. Latency is the *time* that elapses between the stimulus and the _____. _____ is measured, rather than responses.

   response; Time

120. The more a child likes the circus, the quicker he will respond (positively, negatively) to the question, "Would you like to go to the circus?"

---

positively

121. The lesser the latency the more (positive, negative) the attitude.

---

positive

122. Read the following statements and decide which one is different. Circle the appropriate letter.

    A. How long has it been since you spent some of your leisure time reading poetry?
    B. After you've checked a book on poetry out of the library how long is it until you begin reading it?
    C. If someone invited you to read poetry at a poetry club meeting how would you respond and how long would it take you to make up your mind?

A is different

123. Questions B and C above measure the _____ between the stimulus and the response.

---

latency *or* time

124. Question A above measures time. But it measures the amount of time involved since the subject's (first, last) response. That is a measure of extinction.

---

last

125. Extinction is a measure of _____. But it involves the amount of _____ since the subject _____ making a response.

●-●

time
time
stopped

126. The *more* positive your attitude towards golf the (more, less) time it will take for you to become tired and extinguish your practice efforts.

●-●

more

127. To help make the distinction clear between latency and extinction look at the following pictures.

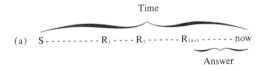

(a)   S ---------- R_1 ---- R_2 ------ R_{last} ------ now

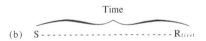

(b)   S ----------------------- R_{first}

Which of the above diagrams, a *or* b, is a picture of latency? What's the other picture?

●-●

(a)   extinction—how long has it been since your last response?
(b)   latency—how long did it take you to begin responding?

128. Let's summarize the four measures we have discussed. Match each measure to its definition

Measure		*Definition*

	Measure			*Definition*
(1)	Extinction	_____a)	The amount of time since the subject's last response.
(2)	Frequency		
(3)	Latency	_____b)	The amount or size of a response.
(4)	Magnitude		
		_____c)	The rate of response during a given time.
		_____d)	The time it took for a response to be initiated.

$\underline{\quad}$ 1 a)
$\overline{\quad}$ 4 b)
     2 c)
     3 d)

129. Identify, using the pictures in frame 127 to help you, which of the following questions measure latency and which measure extinction.

(a) _____ "How long has it been since you wrote to your mother, son?"

(b) _____ "When should we go camping?"

(c) _____ If there weren't any football games on TV how long do you think it would take you to begin mowing the lawn?

(d) _____ How long has it been since you stopped smoking?

(e) _____ How often do you read a fiction book?

(f) _____ How long did it take you to stop smoking?

(a) extinction—how long since the last response

(b) latency—the question was the stimulus and the response will be going camping

(c) latency—same as above except mowing will be the response

(d) extinction—same as (a) above

(e) frequency—didn't your mother teach you not to trust anybody who writes programs?

(f) extinction—same as (a) above

130. Which of the following does not represent a measure to use in attitudinal questions?

   A. magnitude   D. latency
   B. frequency   E. extinction
   C. objective

▄▄▄

   C. objective

131. Match the questions in the right column to the measures in the left column. Do so very carefully.

   Measures   *Questions*

   A. magnitude   _____(1) In an average session how many push-ups do you do?
   B. frequency
   C. extinction   _____(2) If you were given a chance to study astronomy when would you start?
   D. latency
                       _____(3) How long has it been since you've oil painted?

                       _____(4) How many people do you recall encouraging to read Shakespeare?

                       _____(5) When was the last time you tried to talk somebody into joining your church or synagogue?

▄▄▄

   (1) B—see frames 109–117 if you missed that one.
   (2) D—see frames 119–123 if you missed that one.
   (3) C—see frames 125–127 if you missed that one.
   (4) A—see frames 109–117 if you missed that one.
   (5) C—that deals with the amount of time since your last response. If the response to this question was "Never" we could assume that the subject's attitude was extinct—or at least non-existent.

132. You now know four ways to write attitudinal questions. The questions can be used to measure _____, _____, _____, or _____.

----

magnitude; frequency, extinction; latency (in any order)

133. The ultimate test of your ability to understand those four measures is to apply your knowledge. Read each of the following descriptions, then write a test item appropriate to the measure specified. Include the answer choices that you would provide the respondent.

   (a) You wish to know about children's attitudes toward writing stories or anecdotes. Write a test item that would measure the *frequency* of their *active* writing behavior. Ask about it at the *choice* stage.

   _____
   _____
   _____
   _____
   _____

   (b) Use the same context as above but write the item so that it measures *extinction* at the same level and stage.

   _____
   _____
   _____
   _____
   _____

   (c) You want to know if the students in your class will be more concerned about the environment as a result of your instructional efforts. To find out you have decided to ask them about their *passive* behavior at the *experiment* stage.

Relate the question to the school's Ecology Club and measure the *magnitude* of their response.

_____

_____

_____

_____

_____

(d)   Using the same setting as (c) above measure the *latency* of the students' *passive* behavior at the *proselyte* stage.

_____

_____

_____

_____

_____

The words in your test items and answer choices may vary from those shown below. However, the form for the question and the answer choices should be similar.

(a)   Generally, how many times per year have you written a story or anecdote rather than partake of some other leisure time activity?

a. Never	d. Three times
b. Once	e. Four times
c. Twice	f. Five or more times

(b)   How long has it been since you've used your leisure time to write a story or anecdote?

a. Today	d. This month
b. Yesterday	e. It's been more than a
c. This week	month
	f. I never have

(c)   Would you be willing to join the school's Ecology Club?

a. Very unwilling	d. Mildly willing
b. Unwilling	e. Willing
c. Mildly unwilling	f. Very willing

(d) If you were asked to lead a membership drive for the Ecology Club how long would it take you to decide?
a. I'd agree immediately   c. I'd probably not do it
b. I might agree later   d. I'd refuse immediately
(If you had six answer choices for the last test item it merely indicates that you were more creative than the author.)

134. If all your answers followed the format for those shown above go on to frame 135. If you had some difficulty or if you are uncertain about your skill let's try four more test items. Complete them using the same process we employed in frame 133. To make your task easier we'll use the same stage and level all the way through the following situations.
Let's assume that you wish to assess the attitude of your students toward reading the accounts of various American minority groups. Construct questions that would assess their active behavior at the experiment stage.

(a) Item measuring magnitude: _____

_____

_____

_____

_____

(b) Item measuring frequency: _____

_____

_____

_____

(c) Item measuring latency: _____

_____

_____

_____

_____

(d)   Item measuring extinction: _____

_____

_____

_____

_____

●●●

(a)   How many books about American minority groups have
      you read that were not assigned in class?
      a. More than 5   d. 2
      b. 4   e. 1
      c. 3   f. None

(b)   During the last month how many magazines or newspaper
      articles have you read about American minority groups?
      a. None   d. About 3 a week
      b. About 1 a week   e. About 4 a week
      c. About 2 a week   f. Generally, 5 or
                                        more per week

(The above question might lead you to believe that we were
asking about magnitude but the answer choices asked about rate
per week—and that's a measure of frequency.)

(c)   When you were asked to check a book out from the library
      on American minority groups how long did it take you to
      do that?
      a. I did it the same day   d. I did it in about two
      b. I did it the next day   weeks
      c. I did it within the week e. I did it just before the
                                        month was up
                                    f. I never got around to it

(d)   During this month how long has it been since you've read
      a book or article about American minority groups?
      a. I haven't   d. Sometime this week
      b. About a month ago   e. Yesterday
      c. About a week ago   f. Today

Once again your answers may vary from those above. If you need
help in determining whether your test items matched the specified
measure, rereading frame 128 may help. If your test items were
still incorrect review frames 109–132.

135. Remember one thing. The concepts of magnitude, frequency, latency, and extinction are useful in writing different styles of test items. But they are not useful in writing objectives. Don't try to include those words in your objectives.

Go on to the next frame.

136. You will find as you write test items that they make a great deal of sense to you. But occasionally, when you ask a friend to read the items, they just don't seem to communicate your ideas. There are some guidelines for writing items which you may find helpful. One set of criteria is listed below. Read, but don't memorize.

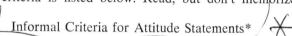
Informal Criteria for Attitude Statements*

1. Avoid statements that may be interpreted in more than one way.
2. Avoid statements that are irrelevant to the psychological object under consideration.
3. Avoid statements that are likely to be endorsed by almost everyone or by almost no one.
4. Select statements that are believed to cover the entire range of the affective scale of interest.
5. Keep the language of the statements simple, clear and direct.
6. Statements should be short, rarely exceeding 20 words.
7. Each statement should contain only one complete thought.
8. Statements [test questions—not the choices or answers] containing universals such as *all, always, none,* and *never* often introduce ambiguity and should be avoided.
9. Words such as *only, just, merely,* and others of a similar nature should be used with care and moderation in writing statements [test questions].
10. Whenever possible, statements should be used in the form of simple sentences rather than in the form of compound or complex sentences.
11. Avoid the use of words that may not be understood by those who are to be given the complete scale.
12. Avoid the use of double negatives.

Go on to the next frame.

* Adapted from Allen Edwards, *Techniques of Attitude Scale Construction* (New York: Appleton-Century-Crofts, Inc., 1957), pp. 13–14.

137. Below are several attitudinal items which the author constructed and inflicted upon defenseless college students. Had the above criteria been rigorously employed none of those items would have been used. Read each of the items and evaluate them in terms of the criteria presented in the previous frame. Write on the lines following each item which criteria or criterion were violated.

A. Social studies can be made interesting and relevant—and I know how to do it.

a. Strongly agree
b. Agree
c. Mildly agree
d. Mildly disagree
e. Disagree
f. Strongly disagree

B. It seems like the best way to make sure things go smoothly is to use a lecture-type setting when teaching.

a. Strongly agree
b. Agree
c. Mildly agree
d. Mildly disagree
e. Disagree
f. Strongly disagree

C. If you were given a chance to try to involve others in a curriculum planning venture, how many people would have to turn you down before you quit trying?

a. Five or more
b. Four
c. Three
d. Two
e. One
f. I wouldn't ask anybody

D. The most interesting thing about teaching reading is the vast number of things which can be done to help a child learn to read.

a. Strongly agree
b. Agree
c. Mildly agree
d. Mildly disagree
e. Disagree
f. Strongly disagree

A—criteria 5 and 7 were violated. The statement was poorly constructed. It would be easier to read if it had been stated as, "I know how to make social studies interesting and relevant for my students."

B—criterion 5 was violated. If you're like most readers you found yourself rereading that statement at least once. It may have been easier to read if it had been stated as, "Teaching goes more smoothly if you lecture."

C—criteria 3 and 6 were violated. Almost no college students could relate to that item. Because curriculum committee membership had little to do with their lives this item measured what some authors have called low-probability behaviors.* Obviously, the item was also too long. Item 5 from the attitudinal pretest, which you took prior to reading the programmed portion of this text, used essentially those same words. Because many of the readers are teachers and graduate students it was decided to retain that item though on those occasions when an undergraduate is the reader criterion 1 is violated by item 5.

D—criteria 1 and 6 were violated. Aside from being too long, it was impossible to tell, if a student marked answer "f," for example, whether he was responding to his own interest level in teaching reading or if he responded to the strategies and materials that he believed could be used to teach reading.

138. The following item was taken from a questionnaire published by a private, nonprofit research and educational organization dealing solely with issues affecting national security.** Read the item and evaluate it in terms of the criteria.

Do you believe that Communists or other revolutionaries should be permitted to hold positions in defense facilities?
Yes ———   No ———

#1—it's difficult to respond Yes or No if you know Communists who aren't revolutionaries. Responses could be made to people who are just communists, or communists and revolutionaries. For some respondents two psychological objects may be being assessed. Responses will be difficult to interpret. Some revolutionary Communists may only demonstrate a passive level of enthusiasm for revolution—they'd rather talk about it than do it.

---

* Lee, Blaine N. and M. David Merrill, *Writing Complete Affective Objectives* (Belmont, California: Wadsworth, 1972), p. 24.

** American Security Council (1101 17th Street N. W., Washington D.C. 20036), *National Security Issues Poll,* April 4, 1972.

139. Read the following test items and evaluate each in terms of the criteria:

A) Would you be willing to take a painting or sculpting course next year?
Criteria violated: _____

B) If you were really bored would you try reading to pass the time?
Criteria violated: _____

C) How many times have you not participated in social studies class discussions?
Criteria violated: _____

D) I would be willing to participate in scientific demonstrations dealing with electromagnetism when I get to the second grade.
Criteria violated: _____

A—#1: that question will confuse respondents who would like to take a painting but not a sculpting class.

B—#3: almost everyone has read to pass the time when bored. Only in very isolated situations would that item provide you with any information regarding a person's attitude toward reading.

C—#5: some readers may miss the word "not" in the above sentence. It should be rewritten as a positive statement.

D—#12: certainly most first-graders will be confused by the word "electromagnetism" even if the sentence is read to them.

140. The next two frames will only be appropriate for those of you who are now or will be involved teaching people who are less than proficient readers. If you do not intend to teach the primary grades or older students with learning disabilities then you can skip those frames.

Need this information? Proceed to frame 141.
Don't need it? Proceed to frame 143.

141.   Primary grade and special education teachers often raise the point that their students have difficulty in reading an attitudinal assessment device. The following procedure may be useful:

(1)   Construct items whose answers tend to be dichotomous, i.e., yes or no, always or never, big or small.
(2)   Read the question to the students.
(3)   Provide an answer sheet similiar to the following:

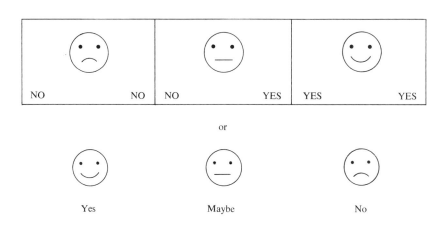

NO NO	NO YES	YES YES

or

Yes	Maybe	No

What's wrong with the second example?

━━━

The "maybe" answer is like a neutral item and will be difficult to interpret.

142.   If you use the above strategy you will need to stress to your students that they must try to be as honest as possible. In this type of test where the students listen to you read it is easy for them to be influenced by your presence and by the reactions of their

_____ .

━━━

peers, classmates, or any synonym

143.   You should now understand how to write attitudinal test items. That understanding should allow you to: (a) identify four types of attitudinal measures, (b) identify specific examples of each measure either from a list of attitudinal items or by writing your own, and (c) use the informal criteria to judge attitudinal items. If there are any of those skills which you believe you still lack return to the appropriate portion in this chapter for a review. If you are confident that you can demonstrate your competence with the objectives stated in the first frame of this chapter then proceed to the next section where you will learn about scoring your test questions.

Chapter 5

Scoring Attitudinal Items

Two of the instructional steps we've previously discussed depend upon your knowledge of the procedures used in scoring attitudinal test items. A dimension of clarity can be added to your attitudinal objectives if you describe the anticipated level of performance in terms of a student score. By describing that expected level of attainment it will be much easier for you to make judgements about revising your teaching or revising your objective. The knowledge you'll acquire in this chapter should, then, aid you in stating your objectives clearly and in making decisions about the necessary revisions.

Scoring items on an attitudinal test is very easy. You will need to learn the answers to only two questions—what value do you assign to the most negative answer, and what values are assigned to the remaining items?

In a very few frames you will have acquired those answers. If you believe that brevity is next to Godliness you will hold this chapter in high esteem.

Behavioral objective:

Given a set of items, the student will devise a scoring procedure that could be used in comparing answers and scores.

Go on to the next frame.

---

144. The curricular plan used for attitudes is the same as that used for cognitive outcomes. Select a goal, state the objectives, select the learning experiences, construct the assessment devices, and revise the teaching plan and/or objectives. In this program we have dealt with two of those five tasks. We'll now deal with, first, scoring items, and second, revising your objective.

Go on to the next frame.

---

145.   Read the following question for the passive level of the Experiment stage:

> Would you be willing to try clay modeling?
>
> | | |
> |---|---|
> | (a) Very willing | (d) Mildly unwilling |
> | (b) Willing | (e) Unwilling |
> | (c) Mildly willing | (f) Very unwilling |

Six levels of attitude can be expressed by a subject. Answer (a) represents a very _____ attitude while (f) is a very _____ attitude.

---

positive; negative

146.   Scores can be assigned to each level. One common procedure is to assign 5, 4, 3, 2, 1, and 0 points to the letters (a), (b), (c), (d), (e), and (f) respectively. In the question in the above frame if a student marked (d) as his answer he would be assigned _____ points.

2—(d) was assigned two points

147.   Look at the following question. Compare the answers to those shown in frame 143.

> Would you be willing to try clay modeling?
>
> | | |
> |---|---|
> | (a) Very unwilling | (d) Mildly willing |
> | (b) Unwilling | (e) Willing |
> | (c) Mildly unwilling | (f) Very willing |

If a subject chose (d) in the above question he should *now* be assigned _____ points.

---

3 (See the next frame for an explanation.)

148.   The rule used in scoring is: the more positive the answer the higher the score. If a subject chose (b) in frame 147 he would be

assigned _____ point because his response is fairly (negative, positive).

1 (one); negative

149. If you were to write an objective for clay modeling you could now be more specific and state, for example, "Upon completion of the introductory class sessions, 80% of the students will score 3 (mildly willing) or higher on the attitude questionnaire." Because more than one question should be used you might want to restate that objective as, "Upon completion of the introductory class session, 80% of the students will demonstrate an average score of 3.0 per item or higher." If a 0–5 scale was used the students' attitudes would be, on the average, (positive, negative) if that objective was met.

positive

150. You will need to decide before your objective is written how many answers you will provide your subjects. For example, read the following objective and its accompanying assessment item.

> Upon completion of the programmed materials, 90% of the students will demonstrate an attitudinal score of 2.

> When you read the program on statistics how did you react?
> (a)   Very favorably   (c)   Unfavorably
> (b)   Favorably   (d)   Very unfavorably

To reach the objective 90% of the students would need to select from the answer choices lettered _____ or _____ __ above.

(a); (b) (Item (d) would be scored 0 and (c) 1.)

151. The answers (a) through (d) would be assigned points on a (3–0, 0–3) basis.

3–0

152.   You could have one question with six responses available to the subject and a second question with four responses. A score of 3 on the first question would be the lowest positive response while a score of _____ on the second question would be the highest positive response.

━━━

3 (That one was tricky. Look again at the items in frames 147 and 150 if you are still confused.)

153.   When you write objectives for attitudes you will need to be very careful in your selection of the verb. You will find that the words "state" and "select" are of great use in writing objectives. However, in frames 149 and 150 the verbs used were "score" and "demonstrate." Try writing an objective for a math class. Use the second level of the second stage.

_____

_____

_____

━━━

Two examples:
1.   The students will state that they have chosen to work some math problems rather than partake in another free-time activity.
2.   More than half of the students will score higher on a post-test when asked if they have chosen to read about famous mathematicians rather than about other topics.

154.   If you found as a result of a pretest analysis that your class had a particularly negative score you might be satisfied with a change to only a moderately negative average score. If a class, on the average, stated that they were very unwilling to try oil painting a significant gain might be to get them to state a *mild* unwillingness. You must choose your own goal when writing objectives.

Go on to the next frame.

━━━

155. After you have taught and you have assessed your students' attitudes you may find that your objective was not met. There are several possible things to consider when you begin the revision process.

(1) Was my goal too high?

(2) Was my teaching ineffective?

(3) Did my test actually measure my objective?

Suppose you had this as your *objective:* "All the students will indicate that they will be very willing to listen to William F. Buckley speak."

Suppose you asked this *test question:* "Would you enjoy hearing William F. Buckley speak rather than go out to recess?"

Suppose you got these *results:* very unwilling—50%, unwilling—20%, mildly unwilling—15%, mildly willing—10%, willing—5%, and very willing—none.

How would you explain those results?

Several things may have been wrong.

(1) Only one question was asked.

(2) The goal was too high.

(3) The question didn't assess the objective. The objective asked for a willingness to experiment while the question asked for a willingness to make a choice. The test item lacked validity.

156. You should now be ready to score a set of demonstration test items. If you're not sure that you could score a set of items with 4, 5, or 6 answers then you will need to reread most of this chapter. If you're confident that you understand scoring then go on to the next frame.

---

157. Revision of objectives, teaching, and tests requires analysis and judgement. The next chapter will provide you with an opportunity to practice those skills while learning about a new topic.

Go on to the next chapter.

Chapter 6

Assessing Self-attitudes

One of the contemporary areas of concern in American education is that of the self-concept. The child's perception of himself is widely agreed upon as being a crucial area of concern to educators. Because children tend to respond to the world in terms of their self-concept it seems only logical that a negative or positive self-concept will influence their academic and socio-emotional growth.

A self-concept is an attitude. It is an attitude towards one's own skills, abilities, and potential. A child's attitude toward himself is as complex as his world. The self-concept can be based on the child's evaluation of his *skill* at throwing a ball, drawing, driving a car, or being able to discriminate sounds. Most children probably have a self-concept that deals with, among other factors, their *abilities* in music, telling jokes, and reading. A portion of one's self-perception revolves around the attitude towards one's own *potential,* such as being elected president, going to heaven, or learning to write better poems. The self-concept is the attitude the child holds toward himself concerning the relevant topics within his world.

Some attitudes towards one's self for both children and adults are held strongly, others not so strongly. Most of the readers of this text would have fairly definitive self-concepts regarding their ability and potential for teaching. There are, though, other less important topics within the collective worlds of the readers—such as jousting. You probably have a very ambivalent, easily influenced self-concept of yourself as a jouster. It would be a much easier attitude to change than your view of yourself as a teacher. Though a child's self-concept is complex most of this is susceptible to change during his school years.

If, as a teacher, you tell a child that he is "doing much better in spelling" your comment is intended to influence his self-concept and, ultimately, his spelling performance. Similarly, negative comments are, ideally, designed to provide a student with a more realistic attitude toward his skill, ability, or potential in some school-related area. However, all of us know from experience that negative teacher comments don't necessarily improve performance nor do they necessarily result in a more realistic self-perception. In the complex world of the classroom so many stimuli are being received by each child that it is difficult to infer in what way a child's view of himself may be changing.

Because the self-concept influences a child's academic performance it seems a logical responsibility of teachers to know how the child perceives himself and how that perception is changing. There are many ways to attempt to gain that information. This chapter is designed to provide some methods for assessing the child's self-concept and interpreting the results of such an evaluation.

Behavioral objectives

A.   Given a set of synonyms the student will select at least two which match the term "self-concept".

B.   The student will state the three steps identified in the text which are employed in constructing an attitude scale for the self-concept.

C.   The student will state at least one of the two recommended observations to make during the administration of an attitude scale.

D.   Given a set of data the student will demonstrate two of the recommended methods in comparing an individual's score against those of his classmates.

E.   The student will state at least one source from which to draw constructs when designing an attitude scale for school children.

---

158.   One of the most important facets to consider in the educational process is that of the child's self-concept. The self-concept is the perception a person has of himself, and is made up of many dimensions. My perception or evaluation of myself in terms of dimensions such as athletics, art, beer drinking, brawling, cards and chatting are all components of my _____.

---

self-concept

159.   The child learns his self-concept. Many dimensions of a child's perception of himself are acquired in school. Children often evaluate themselves using school-based dimensions such as math-

ematics, neatness, speaking ability, and leadership. Though a description of a child's learning process in terms of a self-concept is much too complex to state here, suffice it to say that at least a portion of that learning can be attributed to the effect of his teacher(s). If teachers do have an effect it seems reasonable to expect that the impact could be either p_____ or n_____.

_____

positive; negative

160. Some of the teacher's impact on a child's self-concept accrues from personal contact with the child, such as direct reinforcement activities. Other ways in which a teacher exerts influence, consciously or not, on a child's perception of himself are indirect, such as curricular choices. In either case, it seems wise for a concerned _____ to a_____ the degree and direction of influence he exerts on each child's self-concept.

_____

teacher; assess

161. A wide variety of devices are currently available to aid a teacher in diagnosing a child's self-concept. Due to the vast amount of time and resources employed in developing many of those devices, a teacher should consider using an existing scale or technique before deciding to construct his own. The NEA publication, *Improving Educational Assessment: An Inventory of Measures of Affective Behavior** contains descriptions of and methods for obtaining many useful instruments. The book is easy to read and very inexpensive.

Go on to the next frame.

_____

162. You may decide, however, that none of the available scales are suitable for your students or that the scales are too difficult to obtain. In the event that one of those contingencies may occur,

_____

* Published by the Association for Supervision and Curriculum Development, NEA, 1201 Sixteenth St., N. W., Washington, D.C. 20036, 1969.

the following frames should be most helpful. The next frames will deal with constructing an attitude scale for your own students. We'll discuss five steps in constructing a scale to assess the _____-_____.

- -

self-concept

163. The first step in building a device to assess the self-concept of children is to *select constructs*. Constructs are the words you'll use in defining what part of a child's total self-concept you are interested in assessing. For example, you may wish to know something about the child's perception of himself concerning dependence-independence. If that was the topic of interest then you would need to state some constructs for assessment. Because you may not want to know about the child's complete view of himself in terms of dependence-independence you'll need to narrow the field. You might only be interested in his view of himself in terms of his dependent-independent behavior with his parents and his peers. You would then have defined the ball park for assessing the child's self-concept. You intend to assess his perception of his dependent-independent behavior with his parents and with his friends. Those two categories are your _____ for defining dependence-independence.

- -

constructs

164. Now that you have loosely defined dependence-independence in terms of your constructs you're ready to *write items* to assess both of those _____.

- -

constructs

165. Because attitude scales are hard to write, the best advice a beginner can get is to write as many items as possible for every construct you've selected. There are a couple of tricks that you

can employ to expand the numbers of _____ that you
need to _____.

●—●

items; write

166. For example, take a basic item for the construct Peers. You
might construct one like the following:

> I would be willing to go shopping for clothes without
> my friends.

The child's answer would give you one piece of information about
his level of dependence-independence towards his peers. You
should be able to see an easy way to construct another item but
ask about his perception of himself as it relates to his parents.
Write that item on the following lines. _____

_____

●—●

I would be willing to go shopping for clothes without either of
my parents.

167. Now you have two quick items. Such fun! If you're aware
you may have anticipated the next suggestion. Categorize the
above two items as to stage, _____, and level,
_____.

●—●

experiment, passive

168. An easy way to add to the above list of items is to change them
to the active _____.

●—●

level

169. On the following lines, first, change the Peers construct item to the active level then, second, change the Parents construct item

to the active level. _____

_____

_____

_____

_____

---

(1)   I have gone shopping for clothes without my friends.
(2)   I have gone shopping for clothes without my parents.

170. Now you have four items useful in selecting those which you'll use in your final attitude scale. The important thing to remember in writing items is to start with as many as you can. Then select the ones which you think will do the best job of assessing the child's _____ of h_____.

---

perception; himself or herself (No male chauvinist here.)

171. After you have started a pool of test items there are two methods by which you can select those that will be used with the students. First, you can make sure that none of the items violate the Informal Criteria stated in Chapter 4. Second, using only the items left after discarding the Informal Criteria violators you're ready for the "eyeball" test. "Eyeballing," as most of you know, involves inspecting the items to ensure that they will actually measure your selected constructs. If you need only one test item at the passive level for the choice stage and two still remain in the pool, retain the one you judge to be most valid. Once you've completed your selection process the scale can now be _____ to your students.

---

given *or* administered

172. After the scale is ready for the students the third task is to *administer* it. Very little is difficult about administering an attitudinal scale. One thing, however, that you must observe is the action of the students. Ask them not to discuss the scale with others as they complete it. It's very easy to sway children. Consequently, the influence of peer reactions to specific items may cause a child to change his answer. Secondly, make sure that the children feel free to ask you to explain items. If you are asked to explain several items the test and/or the directions are quite probably poor. If you're asked to explain one item by several people you should consider _____ it from your final assessment.

---

discarding (If the question doesn't communicate to your students it's very doubtful that the results will be valid.)

173. When you begin to *evaluate the scale* you'll first score the items. A wise, and time-honored pattern, is to score one item for all students, then the second item for all students, and so on. By employing that procedure you have the opportunity to informally analyze each item. Good self-concept items will generate a frequency pattern like a normal curve. Poor self-concept items are those where all or most of your students will select one answer. If that occurs you should _____ that item.

---

discard, delete—or a synonym

174. After you've evaluated all the items you'll need to get a total score for each student. If you're really enthusiastic you'd even acquire a total score for each of the _____ that made up your _____.

---

constructs; scale *or* test

175. Now that you've calculated total test and sub-test (construct) scores you're ready for the difficult task of *interpretation*. There are many complexities involved in constructing a technically

sound self-concept assessment device. There are more complexities, though, in interpreting the results to a child, his parents, or even for yourself. Following are a few suggestions to aid you in _____ the results of your scale.

---

interpreting

176.   Don't believe that you've measured all there is to know about the child's _____.

---

self-concept

177.   Any test samples from a person's repetoire of behaviors. So will your test only sample. If, for instance, a child scores low on the test, don't tell him he has a negative self-concept. Tell him that the assessment indicated that he seemed troubled, worried, or concerned about having his friends or parents with him. The test merely indicates what a child's perception may be—not what

_____   _____   _____.

---

it actually is—or any other words which state caution in interpreting the test results

178.   Always ask the child if he agrees with your interpretation. The test is not infallible—because you're not. Your interpretation of test scores may be incorrect. If most of your interpretations are correct then the test is probably valid. Validation is gained by checking your information with _____.

---

the child, *or* the child's parents, *or* another source.

179.   Let's use a specific instance. Suppose you acquired the following results for child A on the scale for dependence-independence.

POINTS SCORED

Constructs	Child A	Class Average	Possible Pts.
Parents	8	18	30
Peers	19	19	30
Total Score	27	37	60

If a score of zero indicated a very dependent child then a score of 60 would indicate a very independent child. The above data indicates that the group is fairly _____ while child A is a bit _____.

• •

independent; dependent—reread the above frame if you missed that

180.   Though child A seems to be nearly as independent as the rest of the class he may only be considered independent as far as his peers are concerned. He seems to be placing a great deal of emotional reliance on his _____.

• •

parents

181.   You might even get curious and examine your test to see how the student scored on specific items. Suppose you compared the test items and found the following data for just the parent construct items.

Level	Child A	Class Average	Possible Pts.
Passive	8	10	15
Active	0	8	15
Total Score	8	18	30

Though child A has a very low score on the active portion he does seem to be w_____ to be i_____ of his _____.

• •

willing; independent; parents

182. If, in consulting with child A's parents, they told you that their child didn't want to be away from them what might be a diplo-

matic question to ask them? _____

_____

_____

Something like, "Have you asked your child recently if he would like to go shopping without you?"

183. In other words, test interpretation takes time and effort. Always, you must be careful to ask many questions and state few answers. By asking questions you can validate the r_____ of your _____ assessment device.

----

results; self-concept *or* attitudinal

184. You may now understand the procedures in (1) selecting _____ _____, (2) writing _____, (3) _____ the test to the students, (4) _____ the test items, and (5) _____ the results of the test.

----

constructs; test items; administering; evaluating; interpreting

185. If you do understand those procedures and suggestions then you'll be in a good position to begin writing your own self-concept scales. You may, however, still feel unsure about topics and items suitable for measuring the self-concept. The last frames in this chapter will be devoted to a discussion of other topics you may wish to consider when constructing a device for assessing the self-concept.

Go on to the next frame.

----

186.   Topics around which self-concept assessments are constructed can vary according to the child's cultural heritage. For example, in many Eskimo cultures bravery and hunting are important components of a boy's self-concept. In the Samoan culture boys and girls commonly use athletics as one relevant dimension in valuing themselves. Within the latter culture hospitality is also a highly valued character trait for boys and girls. As a result most Samoan children would have as one dimension of their self-perception the c_____ of hospitality.

construct

187.   In other words, children develop a self-concept related to their _____ heritage.

cultural

188.   If the group of students you're teaching come from a culture that highly values religion then it seems logical that an important dimension of your students' respective self-concepts is that of _____.

religion

189.   One helpful technique then in selecting topics for self-concept assessment is to look at the student's culture. The more important dimensions that make up his self-concept are acquired from those of his culture—his parents, peers, church, and community. To select topics and constructs relevant to a class the teacher would do well to examine as closely as he can the child's _____.

culture *or* community

190.   You may, however, find that the generalized topics which de-
        scribe a culture's values are of lesser importance to your informa-
        tional needs. You may wish to know how a child feels about
        himself academically. In that case, an excellent reflection of a
        community's needs may be the curriculum guide for that district.
        Assuming that such a reference was constructed by representa-
        tives of relevant groups within the community the guide should
        mirror the _____ of the community.

        attitudes *or* beliefs *or* values *or* goals *or* needs, etc.

191.   Suppose that one of the goals of the community was to ensure
        that children developed a concern for the rights of others. You
        could interpret that to mean that children would support one an-
        other. One common experience children have regarding a con-
        cern for or a support of the rights of others is with a bully. If
        you wished to assess a child's self-concept as it related to sup-
        porting others you might then ask your students to respond to
        an item like:

              I would be willing to tell a bully to quit picking on one
              of my friends.
              a. Not at all   d. I'd be cautious when I
              b. I'd be unwilling   did it
              c. I'd be hesitant   e. I'd do it
                                          f. I'd be very willing

        Now answer the following questions in order about the above
        item.

        a. What level and stage does it represent? _____

        b. If a child had a positive attitude toward the rights of others

            which answers might he choose? _____

        c. Can you think of reasons why a child might choose e. and f.
            other than having a positive attitude toward the rights of

            others? _____
        d. Can you think of reasons why a child might choose a. and b.
            other than having a negative attitude toward the rights of

others? _____

_____

e. Should you use just this one item in your test to assess a

child's attitude towards the rights of others? _____

f. Why or why not? _____

_____

• •

a. Level—passive; stage—choice (Could be a sacrifice for a
   usually non-aggressive child.)
b. d, e, and f—maybe c.
c. If the respondent was also a bully or, at least, an aggressive
   child this may represent a chance to fulfill his need for
   aggression—not a desire to rectify a socially unacceptable
   setting.
d. If the respondent was a very passive, meek child he may
   have a comparatively strong positive attitude toward the
   rights of others, but due to his pacific nature, he may be
   scared to death of a bully. This item, then, would require him
   to make not just a choice but possibly a sacrifice.
e. No.
f. Validity, the concept of testing what you actually want to
   assess, requires that you base your interpretation on a wide
   range of questions—the setting of the question as well as
   stage and level.

192. For those of you who may need some more ideas for items to
assess a child's self-perception in terms of the topic "the rights
of others," here are a few statements to get you started.

a. I have attempted to listen carefully to my (brother or sister)
   explain (his or her) side in an argument between us.
b. I would be willing to join a group which was attempting to
   increase voter registration.
c. I have written letters to the editor regarding prison reform.
d. If I found a lost billfold I would be willing to return it to
   the school office.

Though each of the above items might fit the category of "rights of others" they each have a different focus. Examine the categorization below:

Item	Focus
a.	Right to speak
b.	Right to vote
c.	Right to fair and humane treatment
d.	Right of personal property

The word "focus" is really just a synonym for what word we've previously discussed? _____

● ●

construct (By choosing the above "rights" we've stated in a clearer fashion what we mean by the "rights of others." *Constructs* are used to *define* the *topic*.)

193. Let's look at one more topic for assessing students' self-concepts. You may decide that "friendship" is a topic which you would like to assess. What would you do first? _____
_____

● ●

Select constructs to define the topic

194. Suppose that you have selected the following as constructs for your assessment of the students' self-concept in terms of the topic of friendship:

a. Friendship toward newcomers
b. Friendship toward peers
c. Friendship toward adults

For construct a. write a test item for the passive level and the

proselyte stage. _____
_____

For construct b. write a test item for the active level and the

choice stage._____
_____

For construct c. write a test item for the passive level and the

experiment stage. _____

_____

Don't worry about providing the answer choices.

•-•

Your answers should be similar in stage and level to the following answers:
a. I would be willing to attempt to convince others to join me in greeting a new person in school.
b. I have given my allowance to a friend who really needed the money.
c. I would be willing to read to one of the old folks in the retirement home.

195. It is hoped that you have a bit of confidence (over-confidence is worse, however) in constructing items to assess self-concept. You should have learned in the above frames each of the following:

a. a definition for self-concept
b. three steps in constructing a scale
c. two observations to make during administration
d. at least two ways to compare an individual's score against that of a class
e. at least one method for selecting constructs

If you don't remember the necessary answers look them up before you continue.
If you do remember them then

Go on to the next chapter.

•-•

Chapter 7

The Soap-Box

Be forewarned: The following section is designed to change your attitude—or at least to instill an even more positive view. If the next chapter is well thought out and well written then you will experience a shift in attitude on a crucial issue concerning education. It is hoped that you will find yourself less negative or more positive toward the topic.

Because you may be ready for an instructional change of pace, the next chapter uses a standard text expository format. Programing is not employed. That change was made only to aid your learning process—not because of a waning faith in programing. A change in an instructional pattern seems to bring about increased attentiveness. Therefore, the following chapter employs a different teaching style.

The specific objective for this segment is stated elsewhere. Don't worry, you'll find it.

If teachers can write objectives for affective behavior and can assess the achievement of those goals, then a crucial question, a very crucial question, must be considered. Given the skill to write affective objectives and given the skill to assess attitudes, should teachers then be held accountable for the affective behavior of their students? If they should, then it is being said that the attitudes and values students express should be used in determining a teacher's worth. If teachers are not to be held accountable for the affective behavior of their students, then it is being said that teachers cannot be judged by the attitudes and values which their students hold.

Historically, just as now, teachers have been expected to foster certain attitudes toward national and community values as well as values toward interpersonal relationships. Though the public can sometimes act as if the schools are the sole institution responsible for the affective development of children, collectively and individually they know better. The attitudes of all of us are shaped by our total environment. Teachers and the public know that. There is, however, no doubt that we as educators have accepted, by employing the state or local curriculum, the responsibility to attempt to influence many of our pupils' attitudes. Not only do we as educators have the right, we also have the responsibility to foster the affective behavior of our students. The nub of the problem becomes clearer. We are expected to facilitate affective growth which is consistent with the goals of the community and those of our individual consciences.

Teachers should be held accountable for their students' attitudes and values. Yet it has been pointed out that almost every adult knows that no one person or institution or event is the sole causal agent for the sum of a child's affective behavior. Given such a complex world and such a slippery topic as affect, it is facetious to say that your appreciation of baseball, for example, was solely the result of your fourth grade teacher's interest in the sport. Undoubtedly, many children enjoy baseball for a variety of reasons other than just modeling teacher tastes. Yet (that word again) are not many children's attitudes toward baseball influenced tremendously by their teachers? Of course they are. As a parent and/or a taxpayer are you willing to ignore the effect teachers may have on your children? If teachers have an effect, and they do, should not the effect be toward the desired goals of your community? Are, then, teachers to be allowed to be unaccountable for the affective behaviors which they foster?

When people learn about something, such as arithmetic, they are assumed to be acquiring knowledge or a skill. If you refine your ability to solve long division problems by attaining a greater degree of accuracy you are said to be learning. But as many of you can remember, those pages and pages of problems where you were to "divide and check your work by multiplying" also elicited an attitude. Your appreciation of long division decreased faster than your skill in dividing increased. In other words, while you learned cognitively, you also learned attitudinally. Much the same thing happens in every subject and skill area. Some people learn to like art as they learn more about it. Some learn to hate diagraming sentences even as they learn how to make the patterns more complex. Attitudes are learned whenever content is taught.

If teachers affect children's attitudes through the content they teach and by the behaviors they demonstrate either consciously or unconsciously, then it seems reasonable to assess that impact. Because we as educators have a responsibility to the community, to the children, and to our own ideals it seems logical to identify as clearly and specifically as possible to all concerned the degree of influence that is being exerted. There seems little doubt that if the techniques are at hand for assessing the attitudinal learning of pupils then such evaluation should occur. Within limits, which will be discussed below, a person of professional integrity should not only accept the role of being held accountable, he should expect affective accountability to become a responsibility of educators.

Accountable for What?

Being held responsible for developing more positive attitudes in students is for many teachers a frightening prospect. Many teachers would become quite defensive at the mere thought of being held accountable for the attitudes of that "little devil in the back of the room." Obviously, there is every reason to be worried and anxious about such a task. But the attitudes of children cannot be ignored. They must be dealt with. In the next pages a few suggestions will be stated to aid those who may be willing but unsure how to proceed. So few concrete answers are known as to how to best plan for, teach, and assess affect that the suggestions below can only be considered alternatives.

Teachers starting to deal with affective objectives often believe that they are quite distinct from other objectives. They are not. Affective objectives should emanate from the existing curriculum. As you may remember from the discussion above, teachers are held responsible for, among other things, fostering the development of more positive attitudes towards the three R's—reading, writing and arithmetic. When you construct a set of cognitive objectives for a content area you would do well to have at least one attitudinal objective to cover that content area. Using the division example above, you may decide that you would like to have children develop more self-confidence in their arithmetic skills as a result of being able to perform three-place long division. If that was the case you would need to plan teaching activities to enhance the child's self-confidence, reinforce him and assess his level of confidence to determine if the teaching is satisfactory. Affective objectives can be selected from and constructed for existing content areas. No new topics or areas of study must be planned. Attitudes should be planned for and assessed within the existing curriculum. Accountability will be less threatening if the teacher's impact is assessed within content areas with which he has previously worked.

Specific objectives are much easier to work with and achieve than global objectives. For years educators have hoped to instill in students an "appreciation for" a variety of topics. That goal was much too ambiguous, too broad, and too ambitious to be of worth. There is no doubt that many teachers did teach a more positive attitude (appreciation) toward art, music, or some other subject. It's just that it became difficult to express anything more than an opinion rather than an interpretation of information he had systematically gathered from his students. If teachers can employ more specific objectives, then educators can actually acquire information from students to help them better analyze the students' attitudes and values. Specific affective objectives will provide the teacher with a base for planning, teaching, and evaluating. Global objectives provide only a general goal and do little to facilitate planning for improved teaching.

Once a specific objective has been written it sometimes becomes clear that attaining that goal is much more difficult than one might have guessed originally. Returning to the earlier example objective, where the student was to state that he had acquired greater self-confidence in his arithmetic skills, that goal is certainly not going to be obtained in a single class day. Affective objectives differ from cognitive objectives in that they often require much more time to achieve. Love at first sight seems to occur more often in novels than it does in the arithmetic class. Children's confidence in their mathematical ability needs to be built by reinforcement, time to practice, feedback concerning the accuracy of their work, and the use of algorithms suited to their prior learning. Though it is legitimate to expect a child or a class to attain some cognitive objectives within a class period generally little attitudinal growth will occur across one period. It may now become clear why it was stated earlier that for each set of cognitive objectives only one or two accompanying affective objectives need be constructed. Too many affective objectives will only frustrate a teacher who could, given only one or two goals as a focus, attend to his pupils' needs more efficiently.

A wide variety of attitudinal objectives could be selected in an idealistic drive to attain accountability. Yet with limited time to foster positive attitudes certainly not all could be met. Who, then, should make the final selection of affective objectives? It seems reasonable that the teacher should only be held accountable for those affective objectives which he chooses. As long as the choice reflects some of the goals within the school district's curriculum the specific choice of an objective should be left to the teacher. Usually only one person knows the needs of the pupils and their present level of attitudinal development—the teacher himself. It seems only logical to expect the teacher to select his own affective objectives in light of his knowledge. Attitudinal objectives should not be imposed by a supervisory agent. The goals of the school have already been stated, usually quite generally, in a curriculum guide. If the teacher's affective objective, specifically stated, is based upon one or more of those goals then that objective should be sufficient for meeting the need to attain accountability.

Our present skill in assessing student attitudes is quite limited. One of the major limits is the need to attain data quickly and interpret it easily. Those two factors often force teachers to ask for information from students where it is necessary to use a test as the source. Because the validity of such a venture is often hampered by the student's inhibitions it usually becomes necessary to ask students not to identify themselves. In other words, if an attitude scale is given the students are asked not to sign their names. When such an assessment technique is employed only group type objectives can be used. Unless the teacher uses some rather questionable actions and codes the answer sheets he has no means for identifying the current level of attitudinal development of the individual student. Therefore, whenever information about attitudes can best be attained by providing students anonymity, group rather than individual objectives should be written.

Another factor to consider is that of pretesting. Tests are designed to gain information, not just to separate the good guys and the bad guys. It seems logical that if you have a general goal which you hope to attain, its level of specificity can be improved by gaining additional information. A pretest, then, is useful in specifying the criterion level you hope to attain at the end of the course. By determining where students are at their entry you can make a more realistic judgement concerning what the level can be at exit. Pretesting, either formally with an attitude scale or informally via interviews or conversations, can gain information necessary to better judge what you might realistically hope to attain.

Another concept which may be useful in achieving attitudinal accountability for teachers is that of realistic goals. If, after pretesting, it becomes evident that a group's attitudes are negative it may be more realistic to state an objective in terms such as "growth" or "increased scores" rather than attempt to achieve objectives using words like "become *more* positive" or "achieve the 4.0 mean level on a 5 point scale." Fostering attitudes so that students become less negative and possibly more objective (a euphemism for "currently neutral") may be a realistic goal. Teachers should, first, assess, at least informally, the attitudes of the group prior to teaching. Then they should state an achievement level which they believe they can attain via diplomatic and professional efforts. To rigidly state a specific attitudinal goal prior to meeting a group is illogical—just as it is with cognitive goals. State the expected achievement level of an attitudinal objective only after determining the entry level of all the students.

Don't state specific attitudinal goals to a pupil or class prior to the assessment. Attitudinal objectives are not cognitive objectives. When teachers employ cognitive performance objectives they are ethically and logically bound to inform their students what it is they would like them to learn. That informing can take place by providing the students the actual objectives. With attitudinal objectives we defeat our purpose if we tell students that they are to perform certain behaviors consistent with selected attitudes. Attitudinal objectives are not performance objectives in that we will evaluate the worth of a student in terms of his attitudes. Rather, we are assessing our worth. To retain that fine balance between the students' honesty and their desire to please it seems only useful to not state specific attitudinal statements to students.

Alert yet impetuous readers might infer that it is being recommended that students not be informed of the teacher's goals—goals which he holds for *their* behavior. Quite the contrary. It is being suggested that teachers state the goals to the students. The line being drawn is that the specific level of achievement to be attained via the teacher's efforts not be stated. Statements which exemplify the desired level of clarity are, "I would like to have all of you enjoy Bach as I do" or "If we do a good job, you learning and me teaching, you should like math a bit better" or "One of my goals is to ensure the fact that you're more confident driving a car." Those types of statements inform the students of your general goals. They put little pressure on the student to tell you a lie to make you happy. Statements which may place pressure on the student to judge you as well as his attitude towards a school related topic are, "If I've done well you'll all circle 'strongly agree' " or "By the time this course is over if I've done my job properly you'll all score at least 30 points on the scale." Honesty is necessary in stating goals to students. Specificity must be dealt with carefully. Informing students of achievement criteria may make you specifically honest and your students diplomats. Tell them the goals—not the desired achievement level.

The last concept to consider is that of assessing attitudes only by using scales. This chapter has undoubtedly implied that attitudinal scales are to be held in high regard. That regard should not be misconstrued. Scales are only one of many methods by which beliefs, values, and attitudes can be assessed. To state that assessment devices such as the typical attitude scale is the best evaluatory device is illogical. Some scales are useful for only specific purposes, others are quite general in scope, and some, sadly, are entirely useless. Attitudinal scales will provide one type of information concerning the emotional set of students. A teacher should have no greater faith in the diagnostic quality of an attitudinal scale than a medical doctor would have in a stethoscope. Each acquires useful information. Each has its diagnostic limitations. The greatest value in the employment of attitude scales is that they are tools useful in diagnosing a portion of the attitudinal set which students hold. As a result of that diagnostic quality scales become a legitimate tool in achieving accountability. That seems to be of sufficient worth to demonstrate the need for teachers to understand and employ attitudinal scales.

Summary

Accountability in education has been widely discussed. However, little has been stated concerning methods useful in attaining professional acceptance of accountability for students' attitudes. The foregoing chapter has attempted to state a rationale for accountability applied to affective development as well as means by which such a goal can be attained.

Teachers should expect to be held accountable for attitudinal objectives which are derived from the existing curriculum. Specific objectives rather than global ones will bring about a clarity of purpose which should remove some of the stigma from accountability applied to affect. Greater periods of time should be provided to attain attitudinal goals than one associates with the temporal limits of cognitive and skill objectives. A full year of instruction or a whole course should be structured around a smaller number of attitudinal objectives than one would employ for the other domains. Group objectives rather than those for individuals are logical when the assessment device is to be an attitudinal scale. Informing a class of the goals, but not the achievement level, prior to beginning a course or year is highly recommended. Pretesting is crucial to the statement of realistic goals. The use of attitudinal scales is to be based on the knowledge that they obtain only one source of data but information that is, nevertheless, useful in diagnosing emotional sets of youngsters.

Accountability in all realms of education can be achieved. The need to involve teachers in selecting the procedures for implementing accountability of student attitudes has prompted this chapter. It is imperative that teachers evaluate themselves in terms of objectives which are philosophically acceptable. The above procedures may help to attain affective accountability.

Chapter 8

Summary

You should now be able to meet *all* of the cognitive objectives which provided the structure for this text. Read through the following list and check the ones you can perform. If there are those about which you're uncertain reread the listed frames to refresh your memory.

Number	Objective	Check if you can perform	Reread these frames if you can't
1A	The student will select appropriate synonyms for the word *attitude*.	_____	1–9, 17–19
1B	The student will select from a list of multiple choice items a method for assessing attitudes.	_____	33–36
1C	The student will select from several alternatives the statements that provide the most appropriate matching rationale for assessing attitudes and attitudinal change.	_____	9–16
1D	The student will state the two selected categories of human behavior that make up affective behavior.	_____	20–26
1E	The student will state two categorical levels of any attitude.	_____	27–32
2A	The student will list the attitudinal stages sequentially.	_____	38–48, 50–57, 60–64
2B	The student will match attitudinal statements to their appropriate stage and level.	_____	49, 58–59, 65–68

Number	Objective	Check if you can perform	Reread these frames if you can't
3A	The student will demonstrate his knowledge of the interrelationship of the two hierarchies by writing three objectives appropriate for a given level and stage.	_____	78–91
3B	The student will correctly order the steps in planning for, teaching, and assessing attitudinal objectives.	_____	70–77
3C	The student will be able to write attitudinal objectives including all four components.	_____	92–97
4A	The student will apply his knowledge of each of the four selected measures (question types) by choosing from a list matching examples.	_____	100–132
4B	The student will demonstrate his knowledge of the four selected measures by constructing appropriate examples for each.	_____	133–135
4C	The student will employ the informal criteria for attitudinal statements by correctly identifying, when shown an item, two or more criteria that are violated.	_____	136–139
5A	Given a set of items, the student will devise a scoring procedure that could be used in comparing answers and scores.	_____	144–155
6A	Given a set of synonyms the student will select at least two which match the term "self-concept".	_____	158–162
6B	The student will state the three steps identified in the text which are to be employed in constructing an attitude scale for the self-concept.	_____	163–178

Number	Objective	Check if you can perform	Reread these frames if you can't
6C	The student will state at least one of the two recommended observations to make during the administration of an attitude scale.	_____	172
6D	Given a set of data the student will demonstrate two of the recommended methods in comparing an individual's score against those of his classmates.	_____	179–185
6E	The student will state at least one source from which to draw constructs when designing an attitude scale for school children.	_____	186–190

If you can meet *each* of the above objectives then you're ready for the attitude scale post-test. If you can, wait at least two days before you take that scale. When you do take the scale try as hard as possible to be objective.

WAIT!   PLEASE WAIT AT LEAST TWO DAYS
AFTER YOU COMPLETE THE PROGRAM TO
TAKE THE POST-TEST.

POST-TEST

Directions: Tear out the answer sheet that immediately follows this test. Read each item below carefully. On the answer sheet circle the answer that best represents your attitude. Make sure that you mark the answer that corresponds to the item. Try to work as quickly as possible.

----

1. If you were given the chance to listen to a well-known educator discuss affective accountability how long would it take you to decide whether to attend?
    a. I'd say no immediately
    b. A few minutes—and I'd probably say no
    c. I'd think it over a while— but I'd probably say no
    d. I'd think it over a while— and I'd probably say yes
    e. A few minutes—but I'd probably say yes
    f. I'd say yes immediately

2. How many times in the last year have you chosen to read about or discuss attitudinal objectives?
    a. Many, many times
    b. More than 5 but less than 10
    c. Three or four
    d. Twice
    e. Once
    f. Never

3. If you were given the chance to plan your attitudinal objectives how long would it take you until you wanted to quit?
    a. Absolutely no time at all
    b. A few minutes
    c. A half an hour
    d. An hour
    e. A couple of hours
    f. A long, long time

4. How often have you discussed with your peers ways by which to initiate affective accountability in the schools?
    a. More than three times
    b. Three times
    c. Twice
    d. Once—for quite a while
    e. Once—for less than 10 minutes
    f. Never

5. If someone invited you to attend a small group meeting to discuss how to write behavioral objectives for attitudes how long would it take you to decide whether or not to go?
    a. No time—I'd say no
    b. A few seconds—and I'd probably say no
    c. I'd need more information —but I'd probably say no
    d. I'd need more information —but I'd probably say yes
    e. A few seconds—and I'd probably say yes
    f. No time—I'd say yes

6. How long has it been since you discussed with other interested educators the topic of assessing attitudes?
    a. Today or yesterday
    b. 2 or 3 days ago
    c. This week
    d. This month
    e. Once sometime this year
    f. Never

7. How often would you be willing to spend your leisure time reading further about educational accountability?
    a. Not at all
    b. About once a month
    c. About twice a month
    d. About once a week
    e. About twice a week
    f. More than twice a week

8. How many times in the last few days have you used your spare time to read about affective goals?
    a. Many times
    b. A few times
    c. Three times
    d. Twice
    e. Once
    f. Never

9. If your principal asked you to spend part of your free time planning attitudinal objectives how would you respond?
    a. Very unwillingly
    b. Unwillingly
    c. Mildly unwillingly
    d. Mildly willingly
    e. Willingly
    f. Very willingly

10. Once you began reading this text how long was it until you tried to convince another of the value of educational accountability?
    a. Almost immediately
    b. In a day or two
    c. It took several days
    d. I haven't—but I will
    e. I doubt that I will
    f. I haven't and don't intend to

11. If you were asked to lead a teachers' meeting where you were to attempt to convince the staff to learn to write attitudinal objectives how long would it take you to decide?
    a. Immediately—I'd say no
    b. A few minutes—and I'd probably say no
    c. I'd think it over a while—but I'd probably say no
    d. I'd think it over a while—but I'd probably say yes
    e. A few minutes—but I'd probably say yes
    f. I'd say yes immediately

12. How often have you attempted to encourage others to write their attitudinal objectives in behavioral terms?
    a. More times than I can count
    b. Several times
    c. Three or four times
    d. Twice
    e. Once
    f. Never

13. How many times within the last week have you chosen to read about accountability in the schools?
    a. More than three times
    b. Three times
    c. Twice
    d. Once—for quite a while
    e. Once—for a few minutes
    f. None

14. Would you now be willing to read about teaching procedures involved in attaining affective goals?
    a. Very unwilling
    b. Unwilling
    c. Mildly unwilling
    d. Mildly willing
    e. Willing
    f. Very willing

15. How many minutes per week do you now usually spend in planning for the affective development of your class?
    a. More than 2 hours
    b. 1–2 hours
    c. 30–60 minutes
    d. 15–30 minutes
    e. Less than 15 minutes
    f. None

16. Would you now be willing to lead a discussion with your peers who were interested in identifying procedures for attaining accountability?
    a. Very unwilling
    b. Unwilling
    c. Mildly unwilling
    d. Mildly willing
    e. Willing
    f. Very willing

17. I have discussed writing and assessing affective objectives with others.
    a. More than 4 times
    b. About 3 times
    c. Twice
    d. Once—for quite a while
    e. Once—for a few minutes
    f. Not at all

18. If a committee of teachers asked me to help them write attitudinal objectives I'd
    a. Say no immediately
    b. Think it over for a few seconds—but I'd probably say no
    c. Think it over for a while —but I'd probably say no
    d. Think it over for a while —and I'd probably say yes
    e. Think it over for a few seconds—and I'd probably say yes
    f. Say yes immediately

19. How long has it been since you've used some of your leisure time to read further about educational accountability?
    a. Today
    b. Yesterday
    c. Within the last 2–3 days
    d. Within the last week
    e. Within the last month
    f. I haven't

20. Would you be willing to spend your free time studying ways to write behavioral objectives for attitudes?
    a. Very unwilling
    b. Unwilling
    c. Mildly unwilling
    d. Mildly willing
    e. Willing
    f. Very willing

21. I have given up some of my free time to plan for the affective development of my students.
    a. Several hours
    b. Two–three hours
    c. One–two hours
    d. 30–60 minutes
    e. Less than 30 minutes
    f. I haven't

22. How often would you be willing to attend teachers' meetings where you were to try to convince your colleagues to attempt to attain affective accountability?
    a. Not at all
    b. Once in a year
    c. Once in a month
    d. Once a week
    e. Twice a week
    f. As often as it took to get the job done

23. Since you began this text how long did it take you to try to convince another person to learn to write affective objectives?
   a. Almost immediately
   b. In a day or two
   c. It took several days
   d. I haven't—but I will
   e. I doubt that I will
   f. I haven't—and don't intend to

24. Would you be willing to try to convince your principal to initiate an inservice meeting on the use of attitudinal objectives?
   a. Very unwilling
   b. Unwilling
   c. Mildly unwilling
   d. Mildly willing
   e. Willing
   f. Very willing

Be sure that you circled only *one* answer for each of the 24 items.

Read the sheet titled Directions for Scoring Your Attitude Tests now.

POST-TEST ANSWER SHEET

Fill in the lines above. Do not put your name on this sheet.

		Do Not Mark in This Area
1. a b c d e f	13. a b c d e f	a) ————
2. a b c d e f	14. a b c d e f	b) ———— n) ————
3. a b c d e f	15. a b c d e f	c) ———— s) ————
4. a b c d e f	16. a b c d e f	d) ————
5. a b c d e f	17. a b c d e f	e) ———— p) ————
6. a b c d e f	18. a b c d e f	f) ————
7. a b c d e f	19. a b c d e f	g) ———— t) ———— v) ————
8. a b c d e f	20. a b c d e f	h) ———— q) ————
9. a b c d e f	21. a b c d e f	i) ————
10. a b c d e f	22. a b c d e f	j) ————
11. a b c d e f	23. a b c d e f	k) ————
12. a b c d e f	24. a b c d e f	l) ———— r) ———— u) ————

Make sure that you have only one answer for each of the 24 items.

When you have finished, read the sheet titled Directions for Scoring Your Attitude Tests.

DIRECTIONS FOR SCORING YOUR ATTITUDE TESTS

Scoring Your Pretest

1. There are two columns of answers on your pretest. In the left column:
    a. Score the six odd numbered items on a 5–0 basis. Write the score to the left of each item.
    b. Score the six even numbered on a 0–5 basis. Write the score to the left of each item.
2. In the right column:
    a. Score the six odd numbered items on a 0–5 basis. Write the score to the left of each item.
    b. Score the six even numbered items on a 5–0 basis. Write the score to the left of each item.

Scoring Your Post-Test

1. There are two columns of answers on your post-test. In the left column:
    a. Score the six odd numbered items on a 0–5 basis. Write the score to the left of each item.
    b. Score the six even numbered items on a 5–0 basis. Write the score to the left of each item.
2. In the right column:
    a. Score the six odd numbered items on a 5–0 basis. Write the score to the left of each item.
    b. Score the six even numbered items on a 0–5 basis. Write the score to the left of each item.

Calculations—Both Tests

Perform the following calculations for both tests.
Write your answers in the box labeled Do Not Mark In This Area.
1. Place the total of the scores for items 1 & 13 on line a).
2. Place the total of the scores for items 2 & 14 on line b).
3. Place the total of the scores for items 3 & 15 on line c).
4. Follow that same pattern until you have completed lines d)–l). and items 12–24.
5. None of the totals on lines a) through l) should exceed 10 points.
6. Add the scores which you have placed on lines a) through c) and place that total on line n).
7. Add the scores which you have placed on lines d) through f) and place that total on line p).

8. Follow that same pattern for lines q) and r).
9. None of the totals on lines n) through r) should exceed 30 points.
10. Place the total of lines a), d), g), and j) on line s).
11. Place the total of lines b), e), h), and k) on line t).
12. Place the total of lines c), f), i), and l) on line u).
13. None of the totals on lines s) through u) should exceed 40 points.
14. Place the total of lines n) through r) on line v).
15. If your calculations are correct the sum of lines s), t), and u) will equal the total on line v). Correct your work if that is not true.
16. Complete all of the above calculations for both the pretest and the post-test.*

When you have finished both tests turn to the next page.

---

* When you have finished send all your remaining money to the IRS.

INTERPRETING YOUR ATTITUDE SCORES

Four attitudinal objectives were constructed for this text. The attitude scales which you have now completed and scored were organized to assess whether those objectives were met. Three of the objectives and their corresponding constructs are listed below:

Construct	Attitudinal Objective
	As a result of having completed this text the reader will:
Further Study	1. Indicate an increased desire to study further a) attitudinal objectives b) teaching for attitudes c) assessing attitudes
Implementation	2. Indicate an increased desire to use or an increased level of use of attitudinal objectives and assessment procedures.
Accountability	3. Indicate a more positive attitude toward educational accountability regarding affective development Successful attainment of the above objectives will be indicated by at least a gain score of 4 points (post-test minus pretest) on the corresponding sub-test.

The fourth attitudinal objective dealt with the whole issue of assessing and stating affective objectives. That objective is stated below:

	As a result of having completed this text the reader will:
Total test	4. Indicate a more positive attitude toward affective objectives and their assessment by achieving a gain score of 12 points (post-test minus pretest) on the attitude scale.

Now that you've completed the calculations of your test you are ready to find out if the text had a beneficial effect in changing your attitude. To accomplish that complete the table on the next page.

Construct	Calculations	Was your gain score?	*Then the Objective was
Accountability	_____ Total from line s) of post-test Minus _____ Total from line s) of pretest _____ **Gain score for Accountability	> +3	Met Not Met
Further study	_____ Total from line t) of post-test Minus _____ Total from line t) of pretest _____ Gain score for Further Study	> +3	Met Not Met
Implementation	_____ Total from line u) of post-test Minus _____ Total from line u) of pretest _____ Gain score for Implementation	> +3	Met Not Met
Total Test	_____ Total from line v) of post-test Minus _____ Total from line v) of pretest _____ Gain score for Total Test	> +11	Met Not Met

Check with your instructor. He may want to see this sheet and/or your attitude tests.

* Circle the appropriate response in that column. (Reread page 103 if you're unsure of your answer.)

** The Gain Score value could be a negative number. That means that a decrease in attitude accrued.

ADDITIONAL ANALYSIS FOR DATA DISSECTORS

If you enjoy analyzing a test (and, concomitantly, yourself) to the nth degree or if you just enjoy pushing data around, the following activities may be enjoyable. If neither of those characteristics is a part of your personality then skip this section and turn to page 109.

Analysis by Stages

If you're curious to know on which stages you've scored highest you can quickly determine that answer. On your pretest and post-test the scores for the first four stages were calculated.

Stage	Your score
1. Line n) is the total for the experimental stage.	_____
2. Line q) is the total for the choice stage.	_____
3. Line p) is the total for the concurrence stage.	_____
4. Line r) is the total for the proselyte stage.	_____

As was noted in the program, sacrifice stage items don't seem appropriate for an educational setting. As a result, no test items were constructed for that stage.

Analysis of Stages

If the stages are useful in constructing attitude scales then a specific pattern should exist for most people. The scores for each higher order stage should decrease. For example, in the above table your score for the proselyte stage items should be less than the scores for the other three. Your score on concurrence should be less than that for the two stages above it. The score you achieved on the choice stage should be less than that for the experimental stage.

If such was not the case don't worry. You may be an exception or the scale may not be as valid as hoped.

Analysis by Level

There should be a difference in scores between the 12 passive level items and the 12 active level items on each of your tests. The scores for the passive items should be higher than those for the active level. If you would like to calculate that score from your own tests use the following table.

Test	Level	Total These Items	Your Score*
Pretest	Passive	1, 3, 5, 7, 9, 11, 14, 16, 18, 20, 22, 24	_____
	Active	2, 4, 6, 8, 10, 12, 13, 15, 17, 19, 21, 23	_____
Post-test	Passive	1, 3, 5, 7, 9, 11, 14, 16, 18, 20, 22, 24	_____
	Active	2, 4, 6, 8, 10, 12, 13, 15, 17, 19, 21, 23	_____

* No value should exceed 60 points in this column.

If the levels were valid then your score on line one (from the far right column in the above table) should exceed line two; line three should exceed line four.

If the score for the passive items on the post-test are:
1. quite a bit higher than the score for the active items then that can be interpreted as an indication that you'd like to do more with the affective domain than you currently are.
2. equal to or only slightly larger than the active items then it appears that your actions are in accord with your desires.
3. less than the total for the active items something is wrong. The levels may not be valid *or* you've miscalculated *or* you were not very accurate in representing your attitude on the post-test.

Comparisons of the passive scores (pretest and post-test) will indicate the magnitude of gain in your willingness to involve yourself with the affective domain. By comparing the active scores you can acquire an indication of the magnitude of gain in your actual involvement with the affective domain.

Data for Further Analysis

There are many other calculations which can be made in analyzing your test. For example, it is possible to compare items using varying measures (magnitude, frequency, etc.) in the answer choices, to compare responses to items whose first answer choice was negative (assigned a zero) to those items whose first answer choice was positive (assigned a value of five), or to compare responses to a specific stage at the active and at the passive levels. To expedite any further analysis which you might choose to undertake a coding table is presented below identifying five characteristics for each item.

ATTITUDE TEST CODING TABLE

	Pretest	Post-test
1	AEPPM	AEPNL
2	FEANE	FEAPM
3	UEPPF	UEPNE
4	ACoANL	ACoAPM
5	FCoPPM	FCoPNL
6	UCoANM	UCoAPE
7	AChPPL	AChPNF
8	FChANL	FChAPM
9	UChPPM	UChPNM
10	APANE	APAPL
11	FPPPM	FPPNL
12	UPANE	UPAPM
13	AEANF	AEAPM
14	FEPPL	FEPNM
15	UEANM	UEAPF
16	ACoPPM	ACoPNM
17	FCoANL	FCoAPM
18	UCoPPM	UCoPNL
19	AChANM	AChAPE
20	FChPPL	FChPNM
21	UChANM	UChAPM
22	APPPM	APPNF
23	FPANM	FPAPL
24	UPPPM	UPPNM

#1	#2	#3	#4	#5
Construct	Stage	Level	Answer format	Measure
A	E	P	N	L

Constructs

A = accountability
F = further study
U = use or implementation

Stage

E = experiment
Ch = choice
Co = concurrence
P = proselyte

Level

P = passive
A = active

Answer format

P = answer begins with most positive choice
N = answer begins with most negative choice

Measure

M = magnitude
E = extinction
F = frequency
L = latency

TEST: ATTITUDINAL OBJECTIVES AND ASSESSMENT

Directions: Immediately following this test is an answer sheet. Tear it out then fill in the requested information. Write all of your answers on that sheet.

●—●

Multiple Choice: For each of the next three items select the *one* choice that is the best answer.

1. The attitude of another person is
   A. nearly impossible to determine.
   B. determined by inference from observing his actions.
   C. assessed best by way of an attitude scale.
   D. assessed best via short interviews.

2. Which one of the following sets of descriptors is best used in defining the term attitude?
   A. Informally learned; usually emotional responses.
   B. Incorporates the affective domain.
   C. Behaviors.
   D. Usually irrational responses.
   E. Usually learned from the culture formally.

3. Assessing the attitudes of children is
   A. best done by a teacher.
   B. generally too complicated for the classroom teacher to undertake.
   C. necessary because teachers are responsible for attitudinal development.
   D. best done in the schools because teachers exert the major impact on a child's affective development.

Short Answer: Each of the next seven items requires you to write in a short answer. Make sure that you use the appropriate lines on your answer sheet.

4. If a person scored 30 points on an attitudinal test which had 8 items and each item had six choices what would be a succinct (one word) interpretation of that person's attitude?

5. Name at least one source from which you can draw constructs in developing an attitude scale for school children.

6. There are three categories used when interpreting a person's attitude. One of those is the neutral category. What are the other two?

7. Read the following test item, then answer the question below:
    I would be willing to teach school in American Samoa.

        a. Very willing   d. Mildly unwilling

        b. Willing   e. Unwilling

        c. Mildly willing   f. Very unwilling

    Using the scoring procedure previously discussed in the text how many points would answer (d) be assigned?

8. If only four answer choices had been provided in the question above, how many points would be assigned the most positive answer?

9. State the two *levels* most useful in categorizing attitudes.

10. When administering an assessment of the self-concept name at least one observation you should be sure to make.

Ordering: The next three test items will require that you order items. Make sure that you mark your answer sheet as directed in each item.

11. List in order the five additudinal stages. Start with the stage of least commitment.

12. Listed below are steps useful in preparing and evaluating attitudinal objectives. Number them 1–5 on the lines in front of each. Step #1 will be the first thing you should do in preparing to teach.

    _____A. Evaluate student growth.

    _____B. Choose the learning activities.

    _____C. Choose a set (may be one) of values or attitudes to teach.

    _____D. Revise the lesson and/or the objective.

    _____E. State the objective behaviorally.

13. List, in order, the three recommended steps to use in *constructing* an attitude scale for the self-concept.

Matching: Read the following two test items. Using the informal criteria shown below mark in the space provided *two* criteria for *each* item which have been violated.

Items	*Criteria*
_____14. Would you at least be willing to read other fictionalized histories such as *Is Paris Burning, USA,* and *The Confes-*	a) Words such as *only, just, merely,* and others should be used with care and moderation . . .

Items	*Criteria*

sions of Nat Turner in the next year?

_____15. Given a chance, as this year when we studied conservation, how willing would you be to walk through the park?

b) Avoid statements that are likely to be endorsed by almost everyone or by almost no one.

c) Avoid statements that are irrelevant to psychological object under consideration.

d) Each statement should contain only one complete thought.

e) Statements should be short, rarely exceeding 20 words.

Identifications: Fill in the lines for the next two sets of items as directed. Make sure that you use the appropriate blanks on your answer sheet.

16–21   Write the name of the appropriate stage and level for each of the following test items.

16.   I have contributed more than $100 to my political party.

17.   I have spoken at the County Commissioner's meeting to try to get them to enact a zoning policy.

18.   I have read 5 books by James Baldwin.

19.   I would be very willing to attend the Citizen's Advisory Council meeting.

20.   I have used my vacation time to work as a counselor at a Girl Scout camp.

21.   I would be willing to try to enlist the aid of other club members in circulating a petition.

22.   Mark with an X the best two individual descriptors of self-concept from the list below:

A. _____ ideal self   D. _____ own behaviors
B. _____ real self   E. _____ self attitude
C. _____ perception of self F. _____ identity crisis

Analysis:

23.   Below is a set of sample scores from an attitudinal test. State two ways in which you could use those data to compare student A's performance to the other students.

Stage and Level	A	B	C	D	E	Number Possible	Class Total
Experiment—Passive	10	10	8	5	9	10	42
Experiment—Active	9	10	8	4	9	10	40
Choice —Passive	9	10	5	4	9	10	37
Choice —Active	8	4	6	2	9	10	29
Total	36	34	27	15	36	40	148

Combinations:

24–28   Match the measures in the left column to the test items in the right column.

Measure

A.   Extinction
B.   Frequency
C.   Latency
D.   Magnitude

Item

_____ 24.   I would be willing to read a book by A. C. Doyle.
a.   Very willing   f.   Very unwilling

_____ 25.   How long has it been since you have attempted to convince another to vote in a local election?
a.   Never   f.   Yesterday or today

_____ 26.   During an average month how often would you be willing to go swimming?
a.   More than   f.   Never
5 times

_____ 27.   When you were given a chance to go to see the film *Hamlet* when did you decide?
a.   Immediately   f.   Immediately
—I didn't go   —I went

_____ 28.   If you had as much time as you wanted to work on your puppet how long would it take until you wanted to quit.
a.   2 or 3 hours   f.   Less than 5 minutes

29. Change the above magnitude item(s) to a set of frequency items. Retain the same attitudinal level the item(s) originally had. Show the (a) and (f) response choices.

30. Change the above frequency item(s) to a set of latency items. Retain the same attitudinal level the item(s) originally had. Show the (a) and (f) response choices.

31–33   Read each of the situations below. Write an objective which matches the criteria specified in the situation.

31. You would like to have all of your students decide that they would rather play tennis than other recreational sports. If things go well, as a result of taking your course, they would state that they would make that decision about 50% of the time.

32. You believe that your music course is so effective that you are sure that the students will be quite enthusiastic. They will be so excited, you believe, that each will actively try to get several other students to attend the class concert.

33. Prior to the beginning of instruction on local bird life you are uncertain of your effectiveness. If things go well you hope that almost ⅓ of the class will state that they would be, at least, mildly willing to join the local Audubon Society.

34–36   Categorize each of the objectives that you wrote for items 30–32 as to stage and level.

37. On the appropriate lines on your answer sheet write an objective for the following situation:
    You want ¾ of your students to indicate that they have recently attempted to carry on a conversation in Spanish with another student.

38–41   For the objective which you wrote in item #37 complete the following tasks.

38. State the words that identified the performer.

39. State the words that identified the degree of attitude.

40. State the words that identified the behavior.

41. State the words that described the stage and level.

Date _____   Name _____

Section _____

ANSWER SHEET: ATTITUDINAL OBJECTIVES
AND ASSESSMENT

Multiple Choice
  1. A   B   C   D
  2. A   B   C   D   E
  3. A   B   C   D

Short Answer

  4. _____

  5. _____

  6. _____

  7. _____

  8. _____

  9. _____

 10. _____

Ordering

 11. _____

 _____

 _____

 _____

 12.   _____A

       _____B

       _____C

       _____D

       _____E

 13. _____

 _____

 _____

Matching

 14. _____ _____

 15. _____ _____

Identifications

 16. _____ _____

 17. _____ _____

 18. _____ _____

 19. _____ _____

 20. _____ _____

 21. _____ _____

 22. A. _____   D. _____

      B. _____   E. _____

      C. _____   F. _____

 23. _____

 _____

 _____

 _____

Combinations

 24. _____

 25. _____

 26. _____

 27. _____

 28. _____

 29. _____

————————————   33. ————————————

————————————   ————————————

————————————   ————————————

30. ————————————   34. ————   ————

————————————   35. ————   ————

————————————   36. ————   ————

————————————   37. ————————————

31. ————————————   ————————————

————————————   ————————————

————————————   38. ————————————

32. ————————————   39. ————————————

————————————   40. ————————————

————————————   41. ————————————

Make sure that you have answered every test item. Then check your answers against those shown on the page following the Bibliography.

TEST INTERPRETATION

Objective	Criterion Score

The student should have correctly answered item(s):

1A	#2
1B	#1
1C	#3
1D	#6
1E	#9
2A	all of #11 in order
2B	both parts for each #16–21, #34–36
3A	in a fashion similar to that shown for #31–33 and #37
3B	all of #12 correctly ordered
3C	in a very close approximation to that shown for #38–41
4A	#24–28
4B	in a fashion similar to that shown for #29–30
4C	both parts for each #14–15
5A	#4, 7–8
6A	both parts of #22
6B	all parts of #13
6C	using words similar to that shown for #10
6D	using words similar to that shown for #23
6E	using words similar to that shown for #5

BIBLIOGRAPHY: TEACHING FOR
ATTITUDINAL DEVELOPMENT

General

Dyer, Prudence. "Changing Values of Students," *Elementary English,* May, 1972, pp. 697–705.

Frost Joe L. *Early Childhood Education Rediscovered.* New York: Holt, Rinehart and Winston, Inc., 1968. Chapter 6, pp. 319–354, includes a set of five readings dealing with affective development in preschoolers and primary aged children.

Humanizing Education. Washington, D.C.: Association for Supervision and Curriculum Development, 1967.

Mager, Robert F. *Developing Attitude Toward Learning.* Palo Alto, California: Fearon Publishers, 1968.

Martin, M. H. "Building the Slow Learner's Self Esteem," *Today's Education,* March, 1970, pp. 46–47.

Meadows, M. M., Jr. "Attitudes and Values: Ingredients of Good Teaching," *Clearing House,* February, 1971, pp. 377–379.

Willians, Robin M., Jr. "Generic American Values," in *A Sourcebook for Social Studies,* ed. Vincent R. Rogers. Toronto: The Macmillan Co., 1969, pp. 133–141.

Language arts

Elementary Reading Instruction, ed. A. Beery, T. C. Barrett, and W. P. Powell. Boston: Allyn and Bacon, Inc., 1969. Chapter 8, pp. 275–310, is a set of five readings on the teaching of attitudes toward reading and literature.

Reading

Bottel, H. "Do Drag Racers Need to Know How to Read?" *American Education,* October, 1971, pp. 3–7.

Critical Reading, ed. M. L. King, B. D. Ellinger, and W. Wolf. New York: J. B. Lippincott Co., 1967.
    a. "Attitudes and Critical Reading," J. A. Pickary, pp. 70–79.
    b. "Children's Attitudes Toward Reading and Their Critical Reading Abilities in Four Content-type Materials," P. J. Groff, pp. 370–376.
    c. "Effect of the Attitudes of the Reader Upon Critical Reading Ability," H. J. Crossen, pp. 376–384.

Mathematics

Johnson, D. A. and G. R. Rising. "Developing Positive Attitudes," in *Mathematics in Elementary Education,* ed. Nicholas J. Vigilante. London: The Macmillan Co., 1969, pp. 142–150.

Social Science

Anderson, Lee F. "An Examination of the Structure and Objectives of International Education," *Social Education,* November, 1968, pp. 639–647.

Frankel, Jack R. "Value Education in the Social Studies," *Phi Delta Kappan,* April, 1969, pp. 457–461.

Junnell, Joseph. "The Limits of Social Education," *Phi Delta Kappan,* September, 1972, pp. 12–15.

Readings on Elementary Social Studies: Emerging Change, Second edition, ed. J. C. McLendon, W. W. Joyce, and J. R. Lee. Boston: Allyn and Bacon, Inc., 1970.
  a. "Values and the Primary School Teacher," B. J. Wolfson, pp. 360–365.
  b. "Guaranteeing the Values Component in Elementary Social Studies," W. W. Bauer, pp. 366–374.
  c. "A Strategy for Exploring Values and Valuing in the Social Studies," A. A. Clegg Jr. and J. L. Hills, pp. 375–384.

Science and Mathematics*

Dunn, H. "Science Gives Me Joy-feels All Over," *Science Digest,* June, 1971, pp. 30–33.

Sund, Robert B. and Anthony J. Picard. *Behavioral Objectives and Evaluational Measures: Science and Mathematics.* Columbus, Ohio: Charles E. Merrill, 1972. See pp. 51–59.

---

* A monthly feature in *The Arithmetic Teacher,* called "In the Classroom," deals with activities most of which are geared toward enhancing mathematical attitudes.

TEST ANSWERS

1. B
2. A
3. C
4. positive
5. values within the child's culture *or* the curriculum guide
6. positive, negative
7. 2
8. 3
9. passive, active
10. ensure that the test is not discussed during administration *or* do specific items require an inordinate amount of explanation?
11. experiment
    choice
    concurrence
    proselyte
    sacrifice
12. <u>4</u> A
    <u>3</u> B
    <u>1</u> C
    <u>5</u> D
    <u>2</u> E
13. select constructs
    write items
    select items
14. <u>a</u>   <u>e</u>
15. <u>b</u>   <u>d</u>
16. choice, active
17. proselyte, active
18. experiment, active
19. experiment, passive
20. choice, active
21. concurrence, passive
22. C, E
23. by individual total scores *and/or* by stage and level scores *and/or* by class average scores
24. D
25. A
26. B
27. C
28. A

29. Generally, how many times per month do you read A. C. Doyle books?

   A. More than 10   F. Never

30. If you were given a chance to go swimming tomorrow when would you decide?

   A. Immediately—I'd say yes   F. Immediately—I'd say no

31. As a result of completing the tennis course, all students will state that they would be willing to choose tennis for recreation at least 50% of the time.

32. Prior to the class concert, all students will state that they have attempted to convince (3) or more other students to attend that concert.

33. As a result of instruction on local bird life, 33% or more of the students will state that they would be, minimally, mildly willing to join the local Audubon Society.

34. choice, passive

35. proselyte, active

36. experiment, passive

37. As a result of Spanish instruction, 75% or more of the students will state that they have attempted conversational Spanish with another student at least once within the last (*week*).

38. 75% or more of the students

39. at least once

40. will state

41. have attempted (active, experiment)